COACH'S PLAYBOOK

DAVE LARKIN

authorHOUSE®

AuthorHouse™
1663 Liberty Drive
Bloomington, IN 47403
www.authorhouse.com
Phone: 833-262-8899

Published by AuthorHouse 02/25/2022

ISBN: 978-1-6655-4815-1 (sc)
ISBN: 978-1-6655-4814-4 (e)

Library of Congress Control Number: 2022903803

Print information available on the last page.

CONTENTS

1st Quarter

2nd Quarter

3rd Quarter

4th Quarter

Overtime

DEDICATION

Dedicated to Laura, Lyndsay and Luke, with all my love. Thank you for your constant support throughout my coaching career. You've made me a very proud father.

I want to thank my daughter in law, Terin, who patiently read my manuscript and offered excellent suggestions for improvement. This book would have never been completed without her editing and contributions.

INTRODUCTION

I was a kid with a passion for football who ended up coaching the sport for 35 years and I am here to share some insight. The purpose of this book is to share my experiences, philosophy, advice, inspiration and encouragement with coaches, administrators, parents, athletes and believers. In this book I share the importance of goal setting, overcoming adversity, the importance of teamwork, why coach, along with quotes and books that have guided me throughout my career. Most importantly, I will share the importance of faith and prayer throughout life's journey.

Before starting this book, it is important for you to know a brief background about me, as the author.

Not only was I passionate about football when I was growing up, I knew that when my playing days were over, I wanted to coach. I love the game of football. I think it's the greatest sport ever. I love the way it prepares young men for the real world by teaching them teamwork, great work ethic, sportsmanship, unity, and overcoming adversity.

I was a head coach at three different high schools in Michigan. Each school was very diverse from each other and each of them brought hardships, successes and very valuable lessons. At each school, the teams won a conference championship and qualified for the state playoffs. I was named Coach Of The Year at each of the three schools.

As an assistant coach, I was on the coaching staff where the teams won conference championships at two other high schools in Michigan, as well as college. I was inducted into the 'Michigan High School Football Coaches Association's Hall of Fame' as well as the 'Michigan High School Coaches Hall of Fame'. Along with these two accomplishments, I was nominated and selected for numerous other awards throughout my 35 year career.

I've had the great fortune to have been on the winning side of most games and intensely feel the fun and energy that goes with winning. I also know the agony of defeat after being on the losing side of many games. I was offered jobs that I didn't even apply for. On the other hand, I know the gut wrenching feeling of being fired and going through the hardships of divorce. There are far more successful coaches out there than I. I share this information with you for you to understand that my journey has not been easy and I do not have a perfect story.

This book is not about a coach who turned everything he touched into gold or a coach that had a stress-free career where wins were just handed to him. Instead, this book is about the knowledge gained from years of experiencing the ups and downs, highs and lows as a young man who had a passion for the sport of football. That young man had some success and went through many trials, but more importantly wants to share his story with anyone aspiring to coach so that it could possibly guide and encourage them. I have made many mistakes in my life and will make many more. I'm human, just like you. I have done many things that I regret, but I continue to strive to be the best person I can be. I hope you, as a reader, gain at least a fraction of enjoyment from reading this book as I did living and writing it! I thank God everyday for the many blessings he has given me. I couldn't have coached for as long as I did and have the same amount of success without Him.

A special thanks to all the players, parents, coaches, coaches wives, officials, sports writers, administrators, secretaries and custodians that I've had the pleasure of working with over the years. Most of all, a huge thanks to my entire family, who continuously supported me throughout my career.

I've gone by many names… Dave, Lark, son, brother, husband, grandpa, relative and friend. Next to "Dad", I like "Coach" the best!

CHAPTER 1

GOD'S PLAN

"We are God's workmanship, created in
Jesus Christ to do good works, which God
prepared in advance for us to do".
Ephesians 2:10

By my freshman year in high school, I knew of my love and passion for football. I not only wanted to be the starting quarterback during my four years of high school, but I wanted to play in college and ultimately, in the NFL. I worked my tail off so that I could be the best that I possibly could. I pushed myself hard not only in the summer, but in every practice, game, drill and sprint. With my religious upbringing in the church, I knew that I couldn't do it by myself. I needed God's help. So, starting in 9th grade, I prayed this prayer everyday... "God, please help me to be a success in whatever I do, especially football". God answered my prayers.

I did get to be the starting quarterback in high school for all four years. I did get to play quarterback in college for four years. However, I knew that I was never going to make it to the NFL. Since I loved the game of football so much, I decided that the next best thing to playing, would be coaching. As it turned out, I ended up having an extremely successful career in football as a coach. Looking back, I probably should have been more specific in my prayers! Once I became a coach is when I first realized that God's plan isn't necessarily my plan, but HIS plan for me was greater for me than I could have ever imagined. Little did I know that God's plan was for me to coach football for 35 years!

Over 80 billion people have walked the earth and no two with the same fingerprint. We're all wonderfully unique. God has a plan for each and every one of us that's far different than what we could have imagined for ourselves. Over 70% of U.S. citizens don't like their job, 40% **hate** their job. Find out what you're made to do using the talents God gave you and that is what will lead you to success.

About two-thirds of the way through my career, I was in a terrible car accident. I had just started my second head coaching position after having moved across the state. Professionally, things were going great with my teaching and coaching position, but I was struggling personally with my marriage. My small pickup truck had rolled three times as was crushed like an accordion, with a small bubble directly above my drivers seat. I walked away from the roll over with only a few cuts and bruises. The police officer said he had never seen anyone survive a crash like that, let alone be able to *walk* away from it. I knew that God was not finished with me yet. He had bigger plans for my life here on earth. Professionally, I had more young men to coach and hopefully influence in a positive way. I had many more successes, records to be broken along with team and individual awards awaiting. Personally, I grew to understand how fortunate I was to have such a great family and became a much better husband and father. Spiritually, I began a much closer walk with God, appreciating all that he's done for me.

I enjoy reading books about successful football coaches. Several coaches talk about their faith and how God guided them throughout their career. I have always had a tremendous amount of respect for Bobby Bowden, the former head coach at Florida State University. I have read his books, heard him speak and watched him coach. He has strong faith in God and I will be referencing him throughout this book. Here is what he said about God's plan in his book; "Faith doesn't make me perfect, but it sure points me in the right direction. I don't worry as much about what other people think, because I believe God has a plan for my life. God's plan may not be my plan, but I try to trust him and press ahead".

In addition to Bobby Bowden, I recommend some other great books written by Tony Dungy (Indianapolis Colts), Lou Holtz (Notre Dame), Tom Osborn (Nebraska) and Bill McCartney (Colorado). These coaches all have one thing in common. Besides being successful coaches, they all have a strong faith in God. They do not push their faith on anyone, but acknowledge that football is not the most important thing in their lives, their faith is. Each of these coaches have all dealt with trying times and hardships and have each won championships and have accomplished so with class. They have all helped troubled players get through some very difficult times in their lives and they were all excellent role models for the young men they have coached. Each of these great coaches have one common denominator; God.

> "I do believe God has a plan for my life. I believe that with all my heart. It has nothing to do with coaching and winning football games championships. I am sure God has gotten my jobs for me. He hand picked them. He must have because I certainly didn't apply for them."
>
> Bobby Bowden, FSU

> "With God removed from the equation, I have found life to be devoid of real meaning. You simply can't win enough games to satisfy yourself or others. No matter what your profession is, there are always some accomplishments that exceed your grasp."
>
> Tom Osborn, Nebraska

CHAPTER 2

GROWING UP

I grew up in a small town just north of Flint, Michigan called Mt. Morris. Flint has become well known more recently for its water crisis, but had always been a big General Motors town. To me, Flint means family.

I was the oldest of six children born to Jim and Mary Larkin. I had one brother and four sisters. My dad was a mailman in the city of Flint. He was an excellent athlete in high school in both football and basketball. Although my dad was not a good student himself, he always held high expectations for me in school and athletics. He would play catch with me and shoot baskets whenever I asked, but never pushed me to spend more time on any one specific sport. I was very self motivated and wanted to be a great athlete like he had been. My dad had zero tolerance for my siblings and me getting into trouble, fighting with each other, not getting our chores done, or worse, not following my mom's instructions. I remember my dad working a second job installing garage doors after he was done delivering mail, so my parents could afford to take us on trips and cover the costs of being a family of eight. Although my mom told me how proud my dad was of me, he never did. It didn't matter how good of a game I played, he would always point out my mistakes. I felt like I could never please him. I wanted his approval, but rarely got it. He was from a generation where he believed men did not cry. He felt as if men who cried, were weak. He parented like a drill sergeant and many times took out his work, financial and marital frustrations out on me and my siblings. When I was young, he would want to 'slap box' with me. I thought it would be fun and an opportunity to spend time with my dad. The game would always start out fun. Then, each time he would slap me a little bit harder, and a little bit harder, to the point where he was hitting me quite hard. Even though he could clearly see that he was hurting me, he would continue until I would cry and did not want to play anymore. My mom would always get upset with him for taking it too far. His response was that he was trying to toughen me up. Another thing he did to try and toughen me up was to wrestle with me on the living room floor. Again, it always started as a fun interaction with father and son, but he would typically go too far and would not stop until I was in tears. Dinner time was not a positive memory either at our house. Everyone was leery of my dads outburst, especially my sisters. They would routinely end up running to their room crying because dad had teased them too much.

Looking back, I did learn many insightful things from my dad about sports, work ethic and providing for family. However, I also knew that my parenting style would not be like his. As a father, I strived to be much more caring and encouraging than he was to me. People saw my dad as a fun-loving guy who was always smiling, which is a trait that many people say about me. I know the stress of raising six kids wore on him. He was much more laid back after he retired and all of us kids were out of the house. As us kids grew up, got married and had kids of our own, he and my mom loved having all of us together as a family. After becoming a coach, my dad would try to go to every game to watch me coach. I could tell how proud he was of my accomplishments, but he never acknowledged that until after I was retired. Many years later at my nephew's wedding reception, my dad pulled me aside and told me how proud he has always been of me. He told me he was proud from my playing days in high school, college and also my coaching career. He apologized for not telling me sooner. At that time it did not matter that he hadn't told me sooner, because I finally had my father's approval. I had tears running down my cheeks as I felt a huge burden lifted off my shoulders. My dad died a couple of years later.

My mom was a receptionist for two surgeons in Flint. She was a cheerleader in high school and a great student. While my dad never seemed satisfied, my mom was always supportive and loving. After my football games, while my dad would point out my mistakes, my mom would always praise me for the plays I made and tell me how proud she was of me. Being the oldest, I was having different conversations with her than my younger siblings. I learned about positive parenting from her and she taught me to be a better overall person. She was always so kind and caring for everyone around her, even total strangers. She would always be smiling even during tough times. My mom was the most forgiving person I've ever met. She taught me how to treat people right, even if they weren't nice to me. She had been wronged by several people in her life, but no matter what cruel thing anyone might have said or done, she always forgave them.

One story of forgiveness that I will never forget is after her mom died. My mom had been secretly written out of the will by her own sister. My mom and her sister were the only two children still alive born to my grandmother. My mom's own sister had convinced their mother to not split the inheritance between the two of them, but have it all go to my moms sister. The six of us kids, who were all grown adults, along with my dad were furious. My mom took the high road and said that it was only money and that holding a grudge against her sister would only make things worse. Although she wasn't happy at all with what her sister did, my mom forgave her and said that the situation was in God's hands, not hers. My faith was formed and strengthened with my mom throughout my entire life.

My junior year of high school my parents had separated. My dad had moved out and was living with another woman, while my mom was home taking care of six kids. At age 16, I was now the man of the house and tried the best I could to help my mom in any way possible. I was confused and furious with my dad. After about a year, my mom sat all of us kids down at the dinner table and told us that my dad said he was sorry and wanted to move back home. My younger siblings were happy and excited to have their father back, but us older siblings did not want him back after all the hurt he had caused, especially to our mother. My mom said that if she can forgive him, why can't we? This was another valuable lesson learned from my mom, Mary Larkin.

My mom was very fun-loving. She liked referring to herself as "The Virgin Mary", even though she had six kids. My mom rarely drank alcohol, but when she did, which was usually at wedding receptions, she was the life of the party and everyone wanted to be around her. She was well known to dance on top of the tables and make everyone laugh. Even though my mom battled with cancer for several years before it took her life, she never once complained. She was always positive and upbeat right up to the end. She was one of the most amazing people I've ever met and a great influence on my life. I was so proud to have her as my mother, as were all my siblings.

I lived in what we called the "garage house" until I was five. It was a garage converted into three small rooms, living room, bedroom and bathrooms. A side area of the garage was converted to the kitchen. Three kids slept in the bedroom, while my parents slept on a hide-a-bed in the living room. We moved into a new three bedroom ranch just down the road when I was five. Once we had six kids, we all shared a room with at least one sibling.

I grew up playing football, basketball and baseball in the neighborhood, surrounded by cousins. Our parents made us go outside to play and we weren't allowed to come inside unless it was meal time or to use the bathroom. With no such thing as cell phones or video games, we were forced to come up with our own fun. I typically played sports with cousins my own age, but idolized the older ones who played high school sports. Even when we did play ball against some of the older guys, you knew your chances of getting hurt were higher as well as being yelled at to play better. I learned to never let them get to me and try to show them how tough I was playing with the older guys. I was always pretty good at whatever sport I played and enjoyed them all. This is where my interest in sports started along with my dad's input. I remember striving to be the best I could at an early age. We played tackle football with no pads and someone was always getting hurt. You'd just shake it off and keep playing. We played football in a lot where the goal line at one end was a drainage ditch and at the other end it was a cyclone fence. You actually had to touch the fence to score. I chipped a few teeth scoring at that end while getting tackled. I went to St. Mary's Catholic School in Mt. Morris through 7th grade, then attended Mt. Morris Public Schools from 8th grade on.

I was always a very competitive person. I hated to lose. It didn't matter if I was playing on a school team, a backyard pickup game or cards. I remember always having that competitiveness. Maybe it started at the dinner table competing for food with a family of eight. I think it was stoked by knowing how good of an athlete my dad was and I hoped to follow in his footsteps. I also know that watching college and pro games on television made me more competitive because I wanted to be like them. Also, once I started playing for school teams and having success, I loved the compliments and pats on the back from friends and relatives. It made me want to continue to improve. That competitiveness carried over into my coaching career.

I was the oldest of six kids. I had four sisters, Melany, Monica, Brigid and Madelyn and one brother, Jim. We loved and cared about each other very much and still do. We are close in age and at one point, when my mom was only 25 years old, she had five kids ages six and under. We had our share of fights like most siblings, but nothing major. To this day, every time we see each other, we hug. I grew up thinking we had a small family, having only six kids since my dad was one of twelve and most of his siblings had more kids than my dad. His siblings had anywhere from nine to eleven kids. He was from a big Catholic family where three of his sisters were named Faith, Hope and Charity. Faith and her husband, Ed Corcoran had eleven boys (no girls) and named some after the apostles Matthew, Mark, Luke and John. One of my dad's siblings was a Catholic priest.

My dad's side of the family all had attended St. Mary's church in Mt. Morris. My dad and uncles were all ushers at the church. We went every Sunday. We got dressed up, sat together and were very well behaved. It always seemed so odd to see all of my cousins that I played outside with look so prim and proper and well behaved in church. I had the same feelings with my aunts and uncles who I was used to seeing at our house playing cards, drinking and being loud. I attended St. Mary's Catholic School from first through seventh grade and began going to the public school in eighth grade.

By my freshman year in high school, I knew that my favorite sport was football. I loved playing quarterback because I had the ball in my hands on every play, it was the most important position on the field and your teammates count on you to make the plays. I loved being the leader of the team and a valuable part of the team. I loved the hard work, discipline and physicality of the game. There is nothing quite like throwing or running for a touchdown under the lights, it is quite a thrill. I was the starting quarterback from 8th grade through 12th grade along with being team captain.

I worked at a family owned grocery store in town during my junior and senior year of high school. I started out bagging groceries and carrying them out to their cars. I soon became a cashier and I made a whopping $1.50 an hour. My parents did not have the money to lend to me so I had to work to buy a car, put gas in it, buy clothes and have spending money.

After I graduated from college, I taught at my old high school and was a varsity assistant football coach. My brother Jim was on the team as a senior captain and two-way starter. We shared a bedroom after moving back home from college, just as we had done while I was in high school. Not many coaches ever shared a bedroom with one of their players. I loved coaching Jim because he was such a competitor. He was a starting running back and linebacker and was one of the toughest kids on the team. One game, he tackled a kid so hard that he cracked his helmet. You could hear the hit all over the field. I loved watching Jim play because he always gave it everything he had. I was very proud to be his coach, but more importantly to be his big brother. My sister Brigid at the time was a junior and a varsity cheerleader on the sidelines at the football games. Game night was so much fun for my parents as they would be in the stands proud of a son who was coaching, another son was a key player and a daughter that was a cheerleader. Due to budget cuts across the state that year, I was laid off along with many other low seniority teachers.

With no teaching jobs in Michigan, I moved to Florida and was hired to be a math teacher and assistant varsity football coach at Taravella High School in Coral Springs, Florida. I had been to Florida to visit my grandpa several times growing up but this was my first big move. My grandpa was chief of police in the next town over to where I was teaching and he had told me the job opportunities. I flew to Florida for a week, stayed with my grandpa and had five interviews. The best part was that I was interviewing the schools, not the other way around as they desperately needed teachers and coaches. After all of the interviews, I got to pick the school that I most connected with and wanted to coach and teach at. I was quite nervous about moving so far away and after only having been out of college for a year. It was such a great experience and I was working with great coaches and taking in all that South Florida had to offer. Coral Springs was a highly recruited area and I coached against kids who turned to be big time college players, most of whom ended up playing in the NFL. After two years, I moved back to Michigan to coach at my old high school for one year and then was hired by Carman-Ainsworth High School in Flint as a math teacher and assistant varsity football coach. I also was a varsity assistant at Flint Powers Catholic for a couple years before getting laid off again due to more budget cuts which led me to take my first head coaching job almost two hours north in Grayling, Michigan.

Grayling was a smaller school with about 500 students and was the only school in Crawford County. The AuSable River ran thru Grayling with lots of opportunity to kayak, fish, hunt and camp which was right up my alley. It was a beautiful area with great people and plenty to do if you like the outdoors. I was so fired up to finally be a head varsity football coach. This was a dream come true. I moved up there with Terry, my live-in girlfriend at the time, who I ended up marrying the second year there. I had a daughter, Laura from a previous marriage who was only seven years old and lived with her mom in East Lansing, which was two and a half hours away. I am sure there were many people who frowned me not being married and having a child that visited every other weekend, but everyone treated us very well. I stayed there for three years where our teams won the Great Northern Conference championship twice and qualified for the state playoffs. I learned so much about being a head coach during those three years. I learned organizational skills, communication skills with players and parents, play calling, ordering equipment, fundraising, travel plans and the motivation to win.

Not long after, the Flint Carman-Ainsworth's principal, Ralph Baldini, called and offered me the head varsity football position. He said he had liked my knowledge of the game, my competitiveness and they way players responded to me while being an assistant there three years prior and kept track of the success we'd been having in Grayling. Ralph played football at the University of Tennessee. He was very knowledgeable about the game and knew what he wanted in his next football coach. He desperately wanted to see winning teams after they had only won three games in the past two seasons. The previous year, the team had only won one single game. The year before that, the team had two wins the whole season. So, I was back at Carman-Ainsworth. It was a much larger school compared to Grayling having over 1600 students. I was teaching math again, but this time as the head coach. This was a huge step in my career to come back to the area where I had played and had coached as an assistant for several years. I was very familiar with the opposing coaches and teams. It was a great opportunity to take a losing program and try to turn it around.

Our first season we were 6-3, which everyone from the players, to parents, to the entire community, was thrilled about. I told them that it was a good start, but not where we want to be. Our ultimate goal was to go undefeated and win the conference championship. We improved on that record each year going from a team that nobody respected and everyone wanted to play because they knew it would be an easy win, to a team everyone respected and feared playing. I was so proud to be a part of that program.

In our second year back at Carman-Ainsworth, Terry and I had our first child, Lyndsay, in February. A year and a half later, we had our second child, Luke in October. My daughter, Laura was now living with us and had attended Carman-Ainsworth schools from elementary up through high school. I was actually her freshman Algebra teacher. After going undefeated one year and winning the first ever Big 9 Conference championship, along with a few seasons qualifying for the state playoffs, I was offered and accepted the head varsity football position at Jenison High School in Jenison, Michigan.

Jenison was similar in size to Carman-Ainsworth, with about 1600 students, but a much different background of students. At Carman-Ainsworth there were thirty different languages spoken, as it was a very diverse school on the edge of the Flint city limits. On the other hand, Jenison was almost entirely white, middle income, Dutch families on the west side of the state. We moved into a brand new house. Laura was now sixteen and a sophomore at the high school. Initially, this was a tough move for her, but it ended up being a great fit for her. Lyndsay was now five and Luke was only three. Jenison wasn't the most talented team, but had players that worked hard and were very coachable. Jenison played in the OK Red Conference, which is one of the toughest football conferences in the state of Michigan. We won the conference championship there and qualified for the state playoffs several times. We played in the state championship game and won more games in a single season than any team in the school's history.

After having coached varsity football my entire career, I had the great opportunity to coach three seasons at Grand Valley State University, which is a NCAA Division II school in Allendale, Michigan. Grand Valley had an excellent team after having won five National Championships by head coaches Brian Kelly (who became the head coach at Notre Dame) and Chuck Martin (who became the head coach at Miami of Ohio).

I coached the running backs one year and the tight ends the next two under Chuck Martin and Matt Mitchell. Although I never coached with Brian Kelly, he and his staff had recruited several players that I had coached over the years and we have remained friends to this day. I have been down to several practices and games at Notre Dame. It has always great to talk about his journey from winning the first National Championship ever at Grand Valley, to being the all time winningest coach in Notre Dame history. While coaching at Grand Valley, we won the Great Lakes Intercollegiate Athletic Conference each year at and went deep into the national playoffs. It was much different coaching at the college level. First, you were coaching great athletes at every position, who were on scholarship and football was their entire life. Second, was the time commitment. Although I put in many long hours as a head coach at high schools, it did not compare to the time that we had to put in at college level football, especially at the level that Grand Valley had been playing at. After the games on Saturday, we typically did not get home until after midnight Sunday through Wednesday.

I finished my coaching career as the offensive coordinator at Grand Haven High School in Grand Haven, Michigan, where we won the conference championship and broke all the school passing and scoring records. I was also very fortunate to have coached my son, Luke, who played quarterback there along with all of his buddies.

CHAPTER 3

THE POWER OF PRAYER AND GOAL SETTING

I pray to God everyday. I thank him for all He's given me. I thank him for my family, my health, my career and I ask for His help in whatever struggles my family and friends or I may be dealing with.

In 2011, the New York Times published an article claiming that feelings of gratitude have been linked to better health, sounder sleep, less anxiety and depression, higher long-term satisfaction with life, and kinder behavior towards others, including romantic partners.

These are a few of my favorite quotes about prayer:

"Be anxious about nothing, but pray for everything"
Phillipians 4:6-7

"For everyone who asks, receives. Everyone who knocks, the door will be opened"
Luke 11:9-10

"Ask and it will be given to you"
Matthew 7:7

"I can do everything through Christ, who gives me strength"

Phillipians 4:13

"Therefore I tell you, whatever you ask for in prayer, believe that you have received it and it will be yours"

Mark 11:24-25

"God wants to answer your prayers. Favor surrounds you like getting into the drivers seat of a car. All the controls surround you, but they will not work unless you put the key in the ignition. It's about believing in God and asking"

Pastor Duane VanderKlok

"You may ask me for anything in my name and I will do it"

John 14:14

In November of 1988, I resigned as a varsity assistant football coach due to my frustration over how the program was being run and was left wondering if and when I would ever coach again. I was always hearing successful leaders talk about the importance of setting goals and writing them down. I had not yet done so in my career, but now knew that if I did set specific goals, wrote them down and most importantly, prayed about them, that they could be achieved. So, as a young assistant coach, I wrote down these six specific goals and prayed for God's help to give me the knowledge, determination and strength to achieve them.

1. Become a head varsity football coach
2. Win a conference championship
3. Qualify for the state playoffs
4. Take a team to the state championship game with my dad on the sidelines
5. Be voted "Coach of the Year"
6. Be inducted into the Michigan High School Football Coaches Association's Hall of Fame

When I first started coaching, these goals seemed very out of reach. However, all six of these goals I achieved. Some might say it was luck or being in the right place at the right time. The thousands of players and coaches that I have had the privilege of working with played a part in helping make these goals and dreams come true. Why haven't all coaches that have spent the same number of years on the sidelines accomplished the same or more than I have? We were all passionate about the game of football. We all strived to be the best we can be and demanded the same from our players. I firmly believe it is the power of prayer and my faith in God that has allowed me to have such a successful and rewarding career.

I have had numerous trials in my life that have exemplified the power of prayer, but none more powerful than when my mom was dying of cancer. After my mom had been battling with ovarian cancer for a couple years, the doctors said there was nothing more that they could do for her. The doctors recommended hospice care to keep my mom medicated and as comfortable as possible until she passed away. With the cancer spreading throughout her body as she laid in a hospice facility, it was extremely depressing for all of us as her family to see her fading away. It was the end of January and my mom wanted nothing more than to spend one more summer at the lake house, looking out over the water, with my dad, her six children and her grandkids. She had shared her desire to do this with me before going into hospice. As her health continued to decline and with all of us sensing her life was soon going to be over, I chose to look up instead of down. As the doctors acknowledged there was nothing they could do for her, I chose to pray to God everyday.

I prayed that God would give my mom **six more months** to live so she could go back to the lake house and enjoy the beautiful Michigan Spring and Summer one last time. I refused to give up hope, just like I knew my tough mother would not, so I continued to pray that prayer with the faith and confidence that God would come through. Each day, my mom continued to show signs of improvement. I pleaded with her doctor to perform more tests to determine how she could be showing this much improvement. She informed me that they usually stop all testing once the patient is in hospice care. I pleaded with the doctor saying that my mom is obviously improving and could we verify it with some medical testing. She reluctantly agreed.

A few days later in early February, her doctor asked to speak to me because not only was I the oldest, I was the only one currently in her room and I was the one that persisted in getting my mom tested. As I walked into the conference room to discuss my mother's situation with the doctor, my heart sank expecting to hear more bad news. Instead, the doctor looked me right in the eyes and said that she has no medical explanation why, but that my mom's cancer was in remission and she is free to go home! I bawled my eyes out right then and there, still in shock with this news. My mom turned from being admitted into hospice to live out her remaining days as her cancer spread, to her cancer miraculously going into remission and being allowed to go home. This was amazing! Her doctor said that most people are sent to hospice to be as comfortable as they can until they die. My mom was the exception. My mom did go back to the lake house with my dad. She enjoyed every minute that Spring as the flowers bloomed, the leaves were coming out and the birds were back. Her favorite bird was the cardinal. She had feeders out for them and enjoyed their presence at her window. My parent's house had cardinal memorabilia scattered throughout the rooms. My mom enjoyed the warm summer and the frequent visits from us kids and her grandkids. I can't remember ever seeing her so happy as I did that summer. It was a gift from God and we all knew it.

That August, six months to the day after she was discharged from hospice, my mom passed away. Was it coincidental that my daily prayer was for mom to live another six months when she was dying of cancer in hospice? I don't think so. Once again, God answered my prayers. Growing up, each time I was faced with a trail, my mom was the one would always tell me to not worry, but to pray instead.

CHAPTER 4

PHILOSOPHY

My philosophy for life is based on what I call "The Four F's". These are my priorities in life.

1) Faith- Give thanks to God daily for all He has done
2) Family- Spend quality time with them and tell them that I love them
3) Football- Always strive to improve our team and the overall program
4) Friends- Appreciate and enjoy friendships

My kids have heard me say many times, "Be nice to everybody. You can never have too many friends".

My philosophy for football cannot be summed up in one or two sentences because there are so many aspects to the game; winning, losing, attitude, work ethic, teamwork, motivation and more. One of my primary coaching lessons that I have shared with my players over the years in which I firmly believe in, I got from Bob Stoops, who was the former head coach at Oklahoma. He said, "Play hard, play smart, play physical and have fun. None of which requires talent".

I never asked my players to win. I did ask them to give their very best effort and told them that if they did, good things will happen. We might not win the game, but if we gave our best effort and played as well as we can and lost, that's OK. You cannot do any more than give your best effort. Sometimes the opposing team just has better players.

I believe that football is the greatest team sport in the world. Eleven players on the field at a time, with many more back-ups ready when needed. Every player must be ready when called upon. For the non-starters, they never know when that moment will be so they must practice as if they will be a starter. Football prepares you for many aspects of life. It teaches you teamwork, how to have a strong work ethic, discipline, overcoming adversity and the power of a positive attitude. I put a sign up in the locker room that said, "We compete not so much against an opponent, but against ourselves. The real test is this: did I make my best effort on every play? Whether or not we win, I would like our opponents to say that they played a team that was very prepared, very physical and never gave up."

I believe you need to have a supportive spouse and children to be a successful coach. You spend so much time away from them, that they need to understand the time commitment it requires. You also need to make sure you set aside quality time with those you love. My wife, Terry was extremely supportive. I set aside every Wednesday night during the football season for "date night". This quality time was so important for us. When I got inducted into the Michigan High School Football Coaches Associations Hall of Fame, I got a big ring. I thought my wife, Terry deserved a ring more than I did because of her endless support, so I bought her a "hall of fame" ring, which was just an anniversary band with some diamonds in it that she had wanted for quite some time.

My two daughters thought it would be awesome being the head coach's daughters since they would know all the guys on the team. They both said it was more of a curse than a blessing because my players were to afraid to ask them out!

One part of my game philosophy is that if we win the turnover margin, we have a great chance to win the game. Meaning, our opponent has to have more turnovers in the game than we do. Example; if our opponent had three turnovers and we did not have any, that would be a +3 turnover margin for us. Likewise, if our opponent had two turnovers and we had three, that would be a -1 turnover margin. I found these statistics that the NFL uses to compare the turnover margin to the chances of winning the game.

Turnover Margin	Winning Percentage
+3	88%
+2	81%
+1	80%
even	50%
-1	21%
-2	9%

In addition, statistics show that we have an 80% chance to win the game if we accomplish three things:

1) Win the turnover margin
2) Run the ball for over 100 yards
3) Keep the opponent under 100 yards rushing

Defensively, I've always told our players that if we hold the opponent to 13 points or less, we will win the game. Game planning against the opponents offense, I felt we needed to take away what they do best. For example, if they're primarily a running team, take that away by stacking the line of scrimmage and force them to pass. If they like to throw short, quick passes, take that away by playing your defensive backs closer to the line of scrimmage and force them to throw long. As a team you can't stop everything, but you can strategize to take the other team's most successful, basic plays away from them with anticipation. I call it "making them play left handed".

I have always been very competitive. I hated to lose, no matter the circumstance. It didn't matter what I was playing or who I was playing against, I wanted to win. I wasn't a sore loser, I just hated to lose. As much as the most avid fan hates to see their favorite team lose, nobody feels worse than the head coach. As coaches, we second guess ourselves making the right play calls, substitutions, clock management, etc. Early in my career, I viewed losing as being a failure. A short time later, I realized that every Friday night, half of the teams in the state lost and many of them had great coaches. Everyone loses eventually. Not one team wins every game every year. Success is not about *not* failing. If that were the case, no one person or no team would be considered successful. Success is about how you learn from losses, mistakes and adversities. That is what makes you successful. Your career does not define who you are. Your career is simply what you do. Who you are is defined by something much deeper than wins and losses. Who you are can be defined as your character and how you treat others. There are thousands of coaches who did not win championships and who had losing records, but made a profound impact on the lives of their players.

"If your only mission in life is to win football games, you'll never win enough to find fulfillment"

Tom Osborn, Nebraska

"One great life lesson I learned from sports is that no one wins every game and we can win championships even after losing some games"

Tony Dungy, Indianapolis Colts

"I hate losing more than I like winning"

Bobby Bowden, FSU

"Losing tears the heart out of you"

Bo Schembechler, Michigan

From 1969-2007, the University of Michigan was coached by Bo Schembechler, Gary Moeller, and Lloyd Carr. Growing up in Michigan, playing and coaching football, I admired the job all three of them accomplished at Michigan. Here are a few things they said that have been part of my philosophy.

Keys to success from Bo Schembechler:

- Keep it simple, don't get too sophisticated
- Coach attitude everyday
- Be organized and be prepared
- Be disciplined
- Out work them
- Dream of success

- Know your players like a book
- Be true to your own personality
- The most important thing is that your players must know deep down, how much you care about them

Keys to success from Gary Moeller:

- Never be out hustled or out hit
- Whichever team has the least turnovers wins
- Don't talk to me about attitude, show me
- Great leadership (seniors must set the tone)
- Before you can be good at anything, it must be important to you

Keys to success from Lloyd Carr:

- Great leadership
- Self disciplined
- Fundamentally sound

For our teams to be successful, I felt that we needed to concentrate on us and how we can improve, not so much on our opponent. If you were to ask any of my players over the years what the most important play of the game is, they would say, "the next one". I always emphasized "the next one" because in almost every game there are a couple of crucial downs that determine the outcome of the game. You just don't know beforehand which plays they will be. It could very well be the next play!

Although football players may not want to admit it, they do want to be disciplined. They want to be pushed to be the best they can be, otherwise they would not invest as much time as it requires of them. I would typically ask my teams the first week of practice if they want to be coached by someone who is going to push them to be the best they can be or someone who will let them take the easy route? I never had a team that didn't want to be pushed.

I've never been a proponent of trash talking or talking up a big game. I didn't like it coming from our opponents and I certainly didn't want to hear it from our players. Everyone wants to tell you how good they are and what they are going to do. I would always say to our players, "don't tell me what you're going to do…show me". Actions speak much louder than words on and off the field. Like the old saying, "a parrot talks much but flies little". One of my favorite quotes about this is from St. Francis of Assisi, when he said, "preach the gospel at all times and when necessary, use words". When opponents try to intimidate our players by trash talking and taunting, my instruction was always the same. I would tell our players to keep their mouth shut, go out there and out hit them, then get back in the huddle and do it again.

My last thoughts on philosophy include focusing on fundamentals is key. Blocking, tackling and ball security are just a few basic fundamentals of the sport. The word *fundamentals* starts with the word "fun". Players need to have fun. Everybody likes to win, it is fun to win, but you can make practices and meetings fun too. If we, as coaches, don't make it fun, we can not expect the players to enjoy their experience playing football.

Most of the teams I coached were undersized compared to our opponents but size isn't everything. The whale is endangered, while the ant continues to do just fine. We've all heard the saying, "it's not the size of the dog in the fight, it's the size of the fight in the dog". Giving your best effort and never giving up, regardless of your opponent and the score, shows true character and determines success.

CHAPTER 5

TEAMWORK AND UNITY

Team: A group of people constituting one side in a contest or competition; a group of people working together in a coordinated effort.

-Webster's Dictionary

S everal very successful coaches at every level believe the difference between championship teams and average teams is unity. I would agree. Our best teams over the years were very unified. Teams that struggled were not. Team unity is very important, but difficult at times to achieve. It is not easy bringing a group of guys together due to the diversity of the group. Egos, preconceived notions, agendas, and poor leadership hurt the practice of unity. Unity occurs when team members care more about the vision, purpose and health of the team than they do their own personal agenda.

> "It's not the individual players that determine success. It's the team! Nothing is more important than THE TEAM!"
> Bo Schembechler, *(former Michigan coach)*

> "In order to have a winner, the team must have a feeling of unity; every player must put the team first, ahead of personal glory."
> Paul "Bear" Bryant, *(former Alabama coach)*

"Whether we're talking about a sports team, work team, school team, health care team, church team or home-based business team, it's important that we get everyone on the bus and moving in the right direction with a shared vision, focus, purpose and direction. When a team comes together, they are able to succeed together. You're either on the bus or off the bus."

Jim Collins, author of *Good To Great*

"We live in a culture that encourages independence and self-reliance. Joining a team brings out the best of what we have to offer and raises our commitment level. Teams aren't just for sports. Most people are part of at least one team. It could be your family, co-workers, church or service club."

Tony Dungy, *(former Indianapolis Colts coach)*

"If you expect your players to excel, you better have a pretty good reason, and that reason must be the pursuit of excellence. Not for the individual; for the team. You will never get the same level of effort from one man seeking glory as from a group of men pulling for a shared goal."

Bo Schembechler, *(former Michigan coach)*

"Belonging to a team spurs individuals to greater commitment and performance than they could ever achieve on their own."

Bill McCartney, *(former Colorado coach)*

After winning the 1995 National Championship…
"This group illustrates how a team of athletes can accomplish much more than the separate members working individually."

Tom Osborn, *(former Nebraska coach)*

After Michael Jordan crawled from his sickbed to score 38 points in a momentum swinging the Bull's win over Utah in the 1997 NBA Finals, what kept him from collapsing when he could barely stand? He said, "I didn't want to let my teammates down."

The book, "Good To Great", is a #1 bestseller by Jim Collins that I highly recommend for any one aspiring to be a head coach in football or any other sport. The book is base on a five-year study of 28 companies that went from good to great and had sustained results for at least 15 years or more. You may ask, why do some companies (or teams) make the leap to greatness and others do not?

1) Greatness is not a function of circumstance. Greatness, it turns out, is largely a matter of conscious choice
2) First who…then what. First, they must get the right people on the bus, the wrong people off the bus, and the right people in the right seats "People are not your most important asset, the right people are!"
3) Every good to great company maintained unwavering faith that you can and will prevail in the end, regardless of the difficulties
4) The executives did not first figure out where to drive the bus and then get people to take it there. No, they first got the right people on the bus, the wrong people off and then figured out where to drive it
5) Good to great leaders understood three simple truths:
   1) If you begin with "who" rather than "what", you can more easilyadapt
   2) If you have the right people on the bus, the problem of how to motivate and manage people largely goes away
   3) If you have the wrong people on the bus, it doesn't matter, you won't have a great company. "Great vision without great people is irrelevant"

Another great book on teamwork is "The 17 Indisputable Laws of Teamwork", by John C. Maxwell. A New York Times bestseller and he's authored over 25 books on leadership.

1. **The Law of Significance-** Teamwork is birthed when you concentrate on "we" instead of "me"
2. **The Law of the Big Picture-** Only when players come together, give up their own agendas and sacrifice for the good of the team, can a team move up to a higher level
3. **The Law of the Niche-** All players have a place where they add the most value, when the right team member is in the right place, everyone benefits
4. **The Law of Mt. Everest-** As the challenge escalates, the need for teamwork elevates
5. **The Law of the Chain-** The strength of the team is impacted by its weakest link
6. **The Law of the Catalyst-** Winning teams have players who make things happen
7. **The Law of the Compass-** Vision gives team members direction and confidence
8. **The Law of the Bad Apple-** Rotten attitudes ruin a team. Most bad attitudes are the result of selfishness
9. **The Law of Accountability-** Teammates must be able to count on each other when it counts
10. **The Law of the Price Tag-** If everyone doesn't pay the price to win, then everyone will pay the price by losing
11. **The Law of the Scoreboard-** If a team is to accomplish its goals, it has to know where it stands
12. **The Law of the Bench-** There are more bench players than starters. Great teams have great depth. Make sure bench players are able to step up to become starters
13. **The Law of Identity-** "You can do what I cannot do. I can do what you cannot do. Together we can do great things." Mother Teresa
14. **The Law of Communication-** Effective teams have teammates who are constantly talking to one another.
15. **The Law of the Edge-** Personnel determines the potential of the team. Vision determines the direction of the team. Work ethic determines the preparation of the team. Leadership determines the success of the team.

16. **The Law of High Morale-** The four stages of morale:

Poor Morale- the leader must do everything
Low Morale- the leader must do productive things
Moderate Morale- the leader must do difficult things
High Morale- the leader must do little things

17. **The Law of Dividends-** Investing in the team compounds over time

The role of the bench players is huge in football and the coaches determine the confidence of the bench players. The team is every player, not just the starters. With only eleven starters on the field at a time, most teams have far more players on the bench. Due to injuries, suspensions, or poor play, bench players could become a starter at any point in time. Bench players must be ready if the guy in front of them should go down. They need to practice as if they are the starter. Your teammates need to be able to rely on you. It is the coaches responsibility to have the bench players ready to step up with confidence. Even if they don't get into the game, the bench player must practice like he's going to and push the players ahead of him to be better.

T.E.A.M.- **T**ogether **E**veryone **A**chieves **M**ore

CHAPTER 6

MOTIVATION

"Motivation is simple. You eliminate those who are not motivated"

Lou Holtz, *(former Notre Dame coach)*

Motivating high school football players can be difficult. They deal with a wide range of issues such as their background, socioeconomic status and home life. High school boys have plenty on their minds like girls, grades, money, clothes, jobs and future plans for college or a trade. Granted, some players are born very self motivated, but most need and want, that extra push of encouragement. Motivation could come in the form of firing them up, humor, compliments, visualization or simply challenging them to push themselves harder. In addition to football being a very physical sport, football is also a very emotional game. The right kind of motivation at the right time, enhances positive emotions for players. Positive encouragement motivates and makes the players proud to represent their school, family and community. More importantly, motivates them to work their hardest on game night. Here's a list of some things I've done over the years to motivate our players and community.

Motivational speeches
- Can not be done too often as it can lose it's appeal
- Short and powerful
- Timing is everything

T-shirts
- Given to administrators, secretaries, lunch servers, custodians to wear on game day
- Specific game/opponent t-shirts to sell at school
- Football camp shirts for the players
- Weight training/lift-a-thon shirts for the players
- Every year a different slogan for that season
- Direct incentive shirts
- Conference champion shirts
- State playoff shirts

Uniforms
- New game jerseys or game pants
- New helmet decal or new color altogether

Team activities
- Pool party with competitions/games
- Bowling
- Golf outing
- Team camp
- College camps
- 7 on 7 tournaments
- Youth camp run by our players wearing their game jerseys
- Players read to elementary students on game day wearing their jersey
- Incentive awards (each game, season, off season)
- Weekly highlight video
- Season highlight video
- Team poster with slogan, schedule, boosters, etc
- Beach workout
- Team dinner

Parents
- Monday Night Football (watch previous game highlights and preview our next opponent to keep the parents updated)
- Have mom or dad wear opposite color jersey on game night

- Meet The Team Night (under the lights introduce all players in full uniform, review expectations, demonstration and photos after)
- Purchase attire through our "Spirit Pack" to represent our team
- Players pictures on buttons
- Allow parent help with pre-game meal
- Helmet decals for family cars

Fundraisers
- Card Sale (local merchants are listed on a plastic card with discounts)
- 'Spirt Pack' (allows community to purchase football attire)
- Pizza sale

Facilities
- Paint locker room
- Magnetic signs on each players locker with their name and #
- Continue a tradition or start a new one
- Pride Rock (huge rock outside our locker room with championship plaques on it. Players touch it on there way onto the field)
- Change as much as you can if the team has been losing
- Keep traditions if the team has been winning
- Take the field a different way
- Practice on a different field
- Work with the band director to form a tunnel on game night

Practice
- Popsicles after practice
- Watermelon after practice
- Last second field goal for sprints (entire team gathers around our snapper, holder and kicker simulating a last second field goal, if he makes it, no sprints and they mob the kicker, if he misses, usual number of sprints and they all pat him on the back for support)
- Big men run pass routes for sprints (one big guy for every sprint to be run. If we planned on running 10 sprints, have 10 of our biggest linemen run the pass routes. From the 20 yard line, one at a time, each player runs a "go" route into the end zone. I would

throw a perfect pass into the end zone to each player. For every successful catch, one sprint is deducted. Absolutely hilarious, the big guys finally get to catch the ball and the entire team is pulling for them. Great team builder!)

CHAPTER 7

POSITIVE ATTITUDE AND OVERCOMING ADVERSITY

A Harvard Business School study found that there are four critical factors in business: intelligence, information, skill and attitude. The first three make up 7% of success, while attitude alone makes up the other 93%

"Attitude", by Charles R. Swindoll:

"The longer I live, the more I realize the impact of attitude on my life. Attitude, to me, is more important than facts. It is more important than the past, than education, than money, than circumstances, than failures, than successes, than what other people think, say or do. It is more important than appearance, giftedness or skill. It will make or break a company...a church...a home. The remarkable thing is we have a choice every day regarding the attitude we will embrace for that day. We cannot change our past...we cannot change the fact that people will act in a certain way. We cannot change the inevitable. The only thing we can do is play on the one string we have, and that is our attitude...I am convinced that life is 10% what happens to me and 90% how I react to it. And so it is with you...we are in charge of our attitudes."

Adversity - "a state or instance of serious or continued difficulty or misfortune"   Webster's Dictionary

We all face adversity at some point. It's a natural part of life. We've all faced difficulties over the years, some more than others. Many of us have struggled in our childhood, school, college, marriage, finances, jobs, etc. Overcoming adversity is an ongoing struggle throughout any football season. Tough adversities to overcome in football include; injuries, penalties at crucial times, being down at halftime, losing a close game or losing your starting position. These are tough obstacles for any player to get through. I often reminded our players that football is very similar to the journey of life. There will be some crucial, tough times in your life guaranteed. Life is not easy. The first time you tried to walk as a child, you fell. You got up and kept trying. We are born with the natural push to keep going, even when we have failed. You will have problems with your finances, marriage, family and job. Life is filled with bumps in the road. How we choose to handle adversity is what makes us better people. How you respond to adversity determines the type of character you have and ultimately, your success. Do not ever let anyone judge you based on how many football games you win, whether you are a starter or not, or if you had a penalty that could have lost a game. Those attributes of football have nothing to do with the quality of man you are. Always give your best effort and continue striving to improve yourself.

Many times I would use the analogy of a fork in the road after a tough loss or losing at halftime. We can choose to feel sorry for ourselves, quit trying and throw in the towel. Or, we can choose to keep fighting, keep striving to improve, and be confident in who we are and turn things around.

Many famous people have overcome major adversity in their desire to be successful. Here's just a few:

Abraham Lincoln-	Lost most of his elections, was bankrupt twice and had a nervous breakdown
Henry Ford-	Started three car companies, the first two went bankrupt
Thomas Edison-	Tried over 1000 times to invent the lightbulb, was told he wasn't smart enough
Michael Jordan-	Was cut from his high school basketball team

Walt Disney-	Was told he had no imagination
The Beatles-	Were told they didn't have a good sound
Dr. Seuss-	The first children's book he wrote was rejected by 23 different publishers
Beethoven-	Was deaf
Helen Keller-	Was deaf and blind
Stephen King-	His first manuscript to be published was rejected by thirty different publishers before someone bought it

Gary Patterson, former head coach at TCU after being down 31-0 and beating Oregon 47-41 in triple overtime:

"Here is the thing about fighting through adversity, it's not just about the football game, it's about the next forty years".

Mike Leach, former head coach at Texas Tech while losing 35-7 to Minnesota at halftime, then winning 44-41 in overtime:

"We may not be where we want to be, but this still is an opportunity. So now you have this unique opportunity to make history. This can be the most memorable game of our lives or it can be a disaster. We have had a lot of amazing comebacks here at Texas Tech. People thought they were impossible. Are we going to be part of it, or are we gonna be part of the ones that quit because we didn't like the way stuff went and we got discouraged because of the way a play went, so I'm going to hang my head and pout? Well, that plane ain't leaving till the clock says 00:00, OK?

Ultimately how's it going to turn out? I don't really know, except I do know that doing our job is the identity of this place. What team are we? We're going to find out this half. They won the first half. Make sure we win the second half."

Pastor Duane VanderKlok, from Resurrection Life Church where I used to attend, talked about overcoming adversity often. These are some of my favorite things he has said:

- Life is a struggle from the womb to the tomb.
- There will be bad things that happen to you that you don't understand. Keep running to God, not away from him.
- Faith can't stop you from trouble coming, but it will help you get through it.

A saying that I would routinely refer to during tough times was "When things are looking down... look up!"

"When facing adversity, count all blessings and be thankful"

James 1:2

"Forgetting what is behind and straining toward what is ahead"

Philippians 3:13

"But he knows the way that I take. When he has tried me, I shall come out as gold"

Job 23:10

"If you faint in the face of adversity, your strength is small"

Proverbs 24:10

"Success is to be measured not so much by the position that one has reached life as by the obstacles which one has overcome"

Booker T. Washington

"Nothing in life is easy and we will second guess our quest at critical times. Our lives take detours that we didn't plan for, or we get pummeled by disappointments, heartaches and tragedies. Pick yourself up yet again and push on. Follow your dreams"

Tony Dungy, (former Indianapolis Colts coach)

"Nothing motivates you like your own failure"

Bo Schembechler, (former Michigan coach)

"The coaching profession isn't anything but a popularity contest and you're popular only as long as you win"

Bobby Bowden, (former FSU coach)

"One day you're drinking wine and the next day you're picking grapes"

Lou Holtz, *(former Notre Dame coach)*

"The way in which you endure is more important than the crisis itself"

Harry S. Truman, 33rd President of the U.S.

"Life is like football. Once a play is run, you don't get a chance to do it over. You have to live with the results of that play. The only thing you can do is move forward and try to make the situation better"

Tony Dungy, *(former Indianapolis Colts coach)*

"As a leader you have to understand you will face adversity. Your reaction to adversity will determine your success or failure as a leader"

Tom Landry, *(former Dallas Cowboys coach)*

You will have lots of opportunities to quit in your lifetime. Whatever you do, don't quit! Never, never, never quit!

The Paradoxical Commandments, by Dr. Kent M. Smith

- People are illogical, unreasonable and self centered…
  Love them anyway
- If you do good, people will accuse you of selfish ulterior motives…
  Do good anyway
- If you are successful, you will win false friends and true enemies…
  Succeed anyway
- The good you do today will be forgotten tomorrow…
  Do good anyway
- Honesty and frankness will make you vulnerable…
  Be honest and frank anyway
- The biggest men and women with the biggest ideas can be shot down by the smallest men and women with the smallest minds…
  Think big anyway

- People favor underdogs but follow only top dogs…
  Fight for a few underdogs anyway
- What you spend years building may be destroyed overnight…
  Build anyway
- People really need help but may attack you if you help them…
  Help people anyway
- Give the world the best you have and you'll get kicked in the teeth…
  Give the world the best you have anyway

I've dealt with my share of adversity in my coaching career. Like most coaches, I have had to deal with injuries to key players, tough losses, losing seasons, player suspensions and irate parents. Without a doubt, the most difficult adversity for me to have to overcome, was getting fired.

I had been the head coach at three different high schools in Michigan and our teams were successful at every school. I did not apply for any of the three jobs, they sought me out. Our teams won conference championships and qualified for the state playoffs at every school. After coaching eight years at Jenison High School, where our teams won the OK Red Conference Championship, qualified for the state playoffs several times, received numerous awards for leadership, character and coach of the year, I was informed by our athletic director that the superintendent wanted me to resign. I was shocked, hurt and in disbelief. When I asked what I had done wrong and why he wanted me to resign, the Athletic Director (who had two sons that had played for me) claimed he didn't really know, but felt the superintendent just wanted to go in a different direction. My initial reaction was that I'm not going to resign, I've done nothing wrong and if I resigned, I would be lying because it was not my choice. I told the Athletic Director to let the superintendent know that I have no desire to resign and that if he wants me gone, he needed to fire me. I also demanded a meeting to get some answers as to why this was happening to me. The Athletic Director was just the messenger and told me he didn't agree with what's going on, but was asked to deliver the news to me. After wanting to know the reasons for my dismissal, I did meet with the superintendent. In our meeting, he mentioned a couple vague points that were not true. I could see that he did not really have a valid reason for asking me to resign, but after the last season, which we finished 2-7, I figured that he just wanted to make a change. If that were the reasoning behind him firing me, I would have understood. He never told me that, nor gave me valid reasoning. In fact, he kept saying that it has nothing to do with wins and losses.

The season that we had just completed was the most difficult that I had ever been through as a head coach. We started off 2-0. The day before our third game, the principal came out to practice to inform me that the team would be playing without several of our key players indefinitely. We ended up having seven starters suspended. Some players were suspended for most of the season, some for the entire season, because they were caught drinking at a party. My heart pulled for the players that got suspended, they knew that what they did was wrong and against school policy, but more importantly how I felt for how the suspension affected their parents and for the guys not being able to play the sport they loved. I felt even worse for our remaining players, who without these seven starters, knew it would be a very difficult season.

Our team, which was not nearly as talented or experienced as our opponents that year, never gave up. I was so proud of the way they practiced and played each week. There were a few parents who thought that I had lost control of the team and it was my fault that the seven players got suspended. I found out later that not only were there some parents in the superintendent's ear about me coaching, a couple of my other coaches were also. The next few years were very difficult for me as I kept my teaching position and continued to do a great job in the classroom, but also being known as the football coach who had been fired. I made sure to remain teaching as I always had. After all, it wasn't these students fault that I was no longer the head coach.

This period of my life was a tough time for me and my family. I had always been known as this successful football coach for many years and my kids were so proud of me. Now, I was known as being the fired head football coach in the school district they attended. The good news, was that within a week of being fired, the head coach at Grand Valley State University, Chuck Martin, offered me a position on their staff. I'll never forget that day when Chuck walked into the weight room when I was teaching, dressed like a recruiting visit and said, "I don't understand why they let you go. I think you're one of the most well respected coaches in the state. Would you like to come to Grand Valley to coach?" I said yes, and it was a great part of my story.

After joining the staff as the Tight Ends Coach the first season and the Running Backs Coach the next, I was fortunate to be part of two conference championships and national playoffs in Division II. One year we ended up losing in the semifinals and another year we lost in the national championship game. As I was coaching at Grand Valley, I kept a close eye on the school that lost me as the head coach, Jenison. For the following eight years after they fired me, they went through three different head coaches and averaged winning only 1.5 games a year.

I coached two seasons at Grand Valley and was planning to move further west in the state to Grand Haven, Michigan. Grand Haven was where my two youngest kids, Lyndsay and Luke would go to high school. I was offered the offensive coordinator job at Grand Haven, which is in the same conference as Jenison. I coached for Grand Haven against Jenison and Grand Haven won. After, I got a phone call from the Jenison High School principal asking for a meeting with me first thing Monday morning and said that the superintendent was very upset with me. I was still teaching Physical Education at Jenison, while coaching at Grand Haven. In the meeting Monday morning, I was told that the superintendent was furious that I ran the score up on his team. I simply could not believe what I was hearing! First of all, we didn't run the score up, we did win but by only two scores. Second, I'm just doing my job coaching and trying to win, no matter the opponent. The bottom line was that he fired me three years earlier and since then, Jenison had only won one or two games a year. Now I'm coaching at a rival school and beat them. Also, I said to the principal (who once again was the messenger) that my coaching job at another school has absolutely nothing to do with my teaching job at Jenison and would not discuss it any further. As difficult of a time that was for me and my family, it was a valuable lesson. Within a few years of being fired, I was inducted into the Michigan High School Football Coaches Association's Hall of Fame and was elected president of that association.

"After getting fired by Tampa Bay, I was disappointed, displeased and it was a disruption to our family. There are

times when decisions are made that we disagree with but must live with, and over time, we realize that life goes on."
Tony Dungy, *(former Indianapolis Colts coach)*

"We also rejoice in our sufferings, because we know that suffering produces perseverance; perseverance, character; and character, hope."
Romans 5: 3-4

As disappointed as I had been after getting fired, I realized that in my profession as a football coach, it happens quite often. Getting fired happens more so in the NFL or NCAA, but unfortunately is starting to happen more frequently at the high school level. Bum Phillips, former NFL head coach once said, "there's two kinds of coaches, them that's fired and them that's gonna be fired". The more research I did on well known, successful, fired football coaches, the more I realized that I was in pretty good company. Here's a list of some well known ones:

NCAA

Mack Brown- fired by Texas after winning 77% of his games, two SWC Championships and one National Championship

Lloyd Carr- fired by Michigan after winning 75% of his games, five Big Ten Championships and one National Championship

Philip Fulmer- fired by Tennessee after winning 74% of his games and two SEC Championships

Mark Richt- fired by Georgia after winning 74% of his games and two SEC Championships

Lou Holtz- fired by Arkansas. Won 64% of his games. The only coach to lead six different teams to a bowl game. Won one National Championship

NFL

Bill Belichick-   fired by the Browns after five seasons, won six Super Bowls with the Patriots

Andy Reid-   fired by the Eagles after winning 130 games, won Super Bowl with the Chiefs

Pete Carroll-   fired by the Jets and the Patriots, won two Super Bowls with the Seahawks

Tony Dungy-   fired by the Buccaneers, won Super Bowl with the Colts

Each of these coaches listed above had to deal with the gut wrenching adversity of being fired, yet overcame that to become better coaches and people. I write a lot about our players having to overcome adversities, but we as coaches have plenty as well

As difficult as it was being fired, I knew that I would not be able to move on from this chapter in my life unless I was willing to forgive those who wronged me. I realized that by not forgiving and dwelling on the past, I was only hurting myself. Forgiving those who mistreated me was the only way in which I could move forward in my life without the bitterness I was harboring. Pastor Duane VanderKlok at Resurrection Life Church in Grandville, Michigan was one person in particular who helped me get through this tough time. Here are some of his quotes that really helped me understand the importance of forgiveness:

"Unforgiveness is like drinking poison, it doesn't affect the other person, but is slowly killing you inside."

"Forgiveness is about shattering the cycle of revenge, not forgetting but turning it over to God and his judgement."

"In the Lord's Prayer it says, forgive us our trespasses as we forgive those who trespass against us."

"If you've been carrying around a lot of "dirt" in your wheelbarrow, it's time to dump it out."

"Get the junk out of your trunk."

The last quote that I love about forgiveness comes from Pema Chodron, who is an American Tibetan Buddhist and author of several dozen books. She says, "Unforgiveness is like hurling hot coals at your enemy. Some might hit them and they will be hurt…but for sure you will be burned."

Even after the shock, embarrassment and anger I felt after having been fired unjustly, it helped me become a stronger person and better coach. It helped me forgive others easier, which I always had a difficult time with. Although it was one of the most difficult things I've had to deal with, it's just another example of overcoming adversity and moving on with your life, better prepared for other difficult times ahead.

CHAPTER 8

TEACHING AND COACHING

Rather than making career choices on the basis of money, select a career path that you are passionate about. It makes life so great to love your work and a blessing to enjoy it. I could have made far more money in other professions, but I chose to teach and coach, which has been very rewarding. I loved working with young people, helping them learn, pushing them to be their best and watching them have fun. All of these have brought me a lot of joy over the years. I not trade all of my experience teaching and coaching for anything. In my 35 year coaching career, I have been fortunate to have led several teams to the conference championships and state playoffs. I don't view coaching career as just wins and losses. It is something far beyond that. That something is so important that I could not imagine doing anything other than be a coach.

> "I didn't get into this business for the love of money, but for the love of kids. I got into it to coach them, teach them life's lessons, help them out and be there for them."
> Jerry Kill, *(former University of Minnesota coach)*

> "Before you decide what to do, figure out what your purpose is. Then decide what to do, how to accomplish that purpose, not on the basis of money, convenience or

availability, if possible, but on the basis of what you're passionate about."

Tony Dungy, *(former Indianapolis Colts coach)*

"I've received plenty of awards in my life. I like to think of these as tributes to the players, coaches, administrators, alumni and my friends, because without them I would have nothing. When I reflect these days, it's rarely about the plays we called or the games we won. I almost always think about the people I've been able to meet and the friends I've been able to make"

Lou Holtz, *(former Notre Dame coach)*

"We are God's workmanship, created in Jesus Christ to do good works, which God prepared in advance for us to do."

Ephesians 2:10

"Find something you love and go after it with all of your heart."

Jim Abbott, *(former Major League pitcher)*

"People don't care who you are. They need you to care who they are. When you do that, you have enough of a platform to influence lives"

Tony Dungy, *(former Indianapolis Colts coach)*

Mike Leach, who has been the head coach at Texas Tech, Washington State and Mississippi State, wrote a letter to a famous trial attorney when he was working towards his law degree prior to coaching. Leach asked the famous attorney if he loved practicing law and if all of the work was worth it. "He suggested that I carefully consider what exactly consumed me. What did I think about when no one else was around? What did I think about going from the sofa to the refrigerator? I thought about law some, but I thought I should go out and try to become a football coach."

I found the Charles Schultz Philosophy about people that made a difference in your life, to be very enlightening.

Take this quiz:

1. Name the five wealthiest people in the world
2. Name the last five Heisman Trophy winners
3. Name the last five Miss America winners
4. Name ten people who have won either the Nobel or Pulitzer Prize
5. Name the last six Academy Award winners for best actor/actress
6. Name the last ten World Series winners

How did you do? The point is, none of us remember the headliners of yesterday. Every one of them are the best at what they do. However, the applause eventually dies away. Awards tarnish. Achievements are forgotten. Accolades and certificates are buried with their owners.

Here's another quiz. See how you do on this one:

1. Name a teacher or coach who aided your journey through school
2. Name three friends who have helped you through a difficult time
3. Name five people who have taught you something worthwhile
4. Think of a few people who have made you feel appreciated and special
5. Think of five people you enjoy spending time with
6. Name six hero's whose stories have inspired you

Easier? The lesson is, the people who make a difference in your life are not the ones with the most credentials, the most money, or the most awards. They are the ones that truly cared.

In 10th grade, I had a junior varsity assistant football coach, Chris Rundle, who really inspired me to become a football coach. He had been a very successful quarterback in college and really believed in me. He was very knowledgable, but soft spoken and encouraging. He thought I had all the tools to be a great quarterback. I had a tremendous amount of admiration for him. I can think of teachers, friends, relatives and coaches that have inspired me. They made a big difference in my life and sincerely cared about me. The one person in my life that always believed in me, encouraged me, loved me and made the biggest difference in my life, was my mom, Mary Larkin. I did not realize how many things she has taught me about life until after she passed away. She has left me with a greater positive impact on me than anyone in the world.

Five things coaches miss after finally hanging up the whistle:

1. The camaraderie with other coaches and community
2. The competition
3. The kids
4. The relationships with players, coaches, administrators and teachers
5. The strategy and preparation

Doug Samuels, footballscoop.com

Of all the names I've been called, "Coach" is still one of my favorites! I love it when I run into a former player, parent or fan and they call me "coach". Typically, our encounters are usually followed by a favorite memory they have that will forever be engraved in their minds. It is especially rewarding to have former players tell me how much they enjoyed playing for me. It is great reminiscing with them on the great memories and the fun they had. It warms my heart and puts a huge smile on my face knowing that in some small way I was able to make their life more enjoyable.

My three kids, Laura, Lyndsay and Luke at Lyndsay's wedding

With my parents, Mary and Jim Larkin at my Hall of Fame induction

Senior year at Mt. Morris High School

Senior year at Saginaw Valley State University

First year coaching back at my former high school

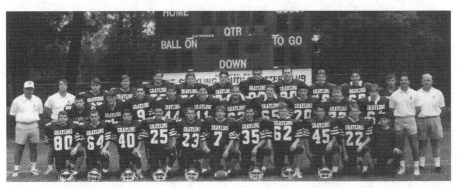

First head coaching job at Grayling High School.
1992 Great Northern Conference Champions

Winning the conference championship at Grayling in the snow

With my parents, Mary and Jim after winning
the conference championship

My dad, Jim and I celebrating after winning
the conference championship

My staff after getting hired as head coach at Flint Carman-Ainsworth

Second head coaching job at Carman-Ainsworth High
School. 1999 Big 9 Conference Champions

Celebrating the first ever conference
championship for Carman-Ainsworth

After winning the Big 9 Championship with my assistant
coaches, Rick Standen, Bill Tucker and Jerry Parker

**2001 DIVISION 2
STATE RUNNER-UP**

Third head coaching job at Jenison High School. 2001 State Runner-Up

After winning the Regional Championship at Jenison High School

Jenison Varsity Football Staff around "Pride Rock"

My oldest daughter, Laura and I after a playoff
win in 2001, her junior year at Jenison

With my three kids, Laura, Lyndsay and Luke after
winning the District Championship in 2001

Jenison High School after finishing Runner-Up
in the State Championship Game

Enjoying a summer sunset on Lake Michigan
with Luke, Laura and Lyndsay

TV interview after a win with Lyndsay by my side

Lyndsay and Luke catching bass while sporting
their Jenison Football sweatshirts

Luke and I after a Jenison win

Jenison High School's upgraded Football Stadium

Tight Ends coach at Grand Valley State University
with Scott Blasco and Jon Matthews

Luke, Lyndsay and I at Grand Valley State

Lyndsay and I after a Grand Haven High School win

Luke and I after a Grand Haven High School win

Down Under Bowl Champions in Australia with my
good friend, Dave Stull and my son Luke, who was our
starting quarterback and named tournament MVP

My dad, Jim and I, enjoying some family time at my sister's cottage

Lyndsay and I at a Notre Dame football game

CHAPTER 9

ADVICE

Advice to assistant coaches

- Be totally loyal to the head coach. If you can't be, resign
- Football knowledge and experience are not nearly as important as loyalty, willingness to learn, being a good teacher, having a great work ethic, being passionate about football and most importantly, caring about your players
- Study successful coaches. Talk to them whenever possible, read books, watch videos, attend clinics and college practices

I think it is crucial to never stop learning, regardless of what profession you're in, along with personal and spiritual growth. I have enjoyed searching through books written by successful coaches I admire to continue learning and improve as a football coach. Here are some of my favorite books along with the coach's name and team:

"Chasing Dreams"	Jerry Kill	*Minnesota*
"Swing Your Sword"	Mike Leach	*Texas Tech*
"Uncommon"	Tony Dungy	*Indianapolis Colts*
"Bo"	Bo Schembechler	*Michigan*
"More Than Just a Game"	Bobby Bowden	*Florida State*
"The Fighting Spirit"	Lou Holtz	*Notre Dame*

"From Ashes to Glory"   Bill McCartney   *Colorado*
"On Solid Ground"   Tom Osborn   *Nebraska*

You can learn to be a better coach by observing coaches you admire. There are some coaches that you have either played for or knew of that you did not like for whatever reason. Maybe they were not organized, disciplined, knowledgeable, positive, caring or committed. You learn how *not* to coach from those people. There are several coaches that you will come across who are doing things the right way and leave a great impression on you. Those are the coaches you can learn to be better from. Here are some coaches that have made a great impact on me and what I have learned from them that have made me a better coach.

Ray Buschemi was the head coach at Taravella High School in Coral Springs, Florida when I was an assistant there after only being out of college for one year. I learned the importance of discipline and great work ethic from Ray. He was very organized and demanded nothing but the best effort from his players. He had high expectations of his players both on and off the field. As a result, the players had high expectations for themselves and the team. Ray spent countless hours watching video tape of our opponents to make sure he was giving our players the best chance to succeed.

Bill Tucker was the head coach at Powers Catholic High School in Flint, Michigan. I was an assistant with Bill for two years before getting my first head coaching job. I learned from Bill how important a positive attitude is for a head coach along with the importance of appealing to the emotional part of the game. He was always positive with the players, regardless of the situation. Whether we were down at halftime, just lost a close game or about to play a team with far better talent, Bill's positive attitude was passed on to our team. Bill coached with great emotion. He was passionate about football, took tremendous pride in coaching those young men and emphasized the importance of carrying on the winning tradition at Powers Catholic. He also taught me the power of visualization and mental imagery. Before each game he would have the players sitting down quietly in the dark, visualizing themselves making great plays.

Brian Kelly became the head coach at Notre Dame, but when I first met him, was the head coach at Division II Grand Valley State. I learned from Brian the importance of preparation, scheming the opponent, practice planning and dealing with the media. He too spent a lot of time watching video, developing a plan to best attack the opponents' defense and then implement that plan throughout the week in practice. He was great at manipulating mismatches with the opponent, getting his best players the ball and attacking the weak links of the defense.

Chuck Martin became the head coach at Miami of Ohio, but prior to that, followed Brian Kelly as the head coach at Grand Valley State. I learned from Chuck how to balance family with football and that making practice tougher than the game, put players in position for better success on game day. Chuck was always a great family man. He loved spending quality time with his wife and two kids. One nigh a week during the season, he would start our staff meeting a couple hours later so he could go home, have dinner with his family and put his kids to bed. He was one of the most demanding coaches I've ever been around. He expected nothing but the best from his players every second of every practice. It would always take the younger players time to adjust to his expectation of perfection. He demanded it every day in practice. When I asked Chuck about his strict demeanor in practice, he told me that he wanted practices to be much tougher than the games. He felt that the games would be easy compared to what the players dealt with in practice. Chuck was always very positive and encouraging with the players on game day. He had great respect for his players, especially the seniors, who had been with him for four or five years. I remember flying back from a national semi-final loss in Missouri and Chuck gave up his first class seat to our senior offensive tackle. Just his subtle way of saying how much he appreciated that players' effort throughout his career.

Jerry Kill was the head coach at University of Minnesota and when we first met, was the head coach at Division II Saginaw Valley State. I learned many things from him. Jerry sincerely cared about every player and coach. He was very humble and usually deflected any praise away from him and towards his coaches and players. He took great pride knowing that he was molding young men for the future.

Tony Annese is currently the head coach at Division II Ferris State University. Tony was a very successful high school coach at four different schools before coaching in college. Tony taught me the importance of having a great relationship with your players. He has an open door policy. Players love to play for him because while he is very demanding, the players totally trust him to have the team prepared every week. I also learned from Tony that you have to have fun. Nobody makes their players laugh more than Tony Annese.

Jeff Quinn was the offensive line coach at Notre Dame. Prior to that he was the head coach at University of Buffalo. Jeff was Brian Kelly's offensive line coach at Grand Valley State, Central Michigan and Cincinnati. I learned from Jeff how to have your priorities in order. He called his the five F's. In order, they were Faith, Family, Football, Friends and Fishing.

I gave my assistant coaches a handout entitled, "What a good coach needs to be"

1. Be a good teacher
2. Know your position and teach the basic fundamentals
3. Be prepared and punctual for meetings, practices and games
4. Constantly seek ways to improve (books, clinics, college visits)
5. Have a positive, upbeat attitude
6. Be loyal to the head coach, staff, players and administration
7. Be demanding of players and have high expectations
8. Help with academic support
9. Willing to help in the offseason
10. Be honest, direct and fair with players
11. Don't succumb to media or parental influence
12. Be a tireless worker

Advice to head coaches

- Be yourself. Don't try to imitate anyone else
- Be disciplined
- Be organized
- Teach fundamentals
- Find something you believe in (offense, defense, special teams)
- Put your players in the best position to succeed
- Surround yourself with loyal assistants

- Expect to win
- Emphasize to players about always giving their best, not winning
- Teach teamwork, sportsmanship, work ethic and overcoming adversity
- Be "thick skinned". Don't take to heart every negative comment
- Be totally honest with players and parents
- Treat players as if they were your own sons
- Spend time with your assistants away from football
- Develop relationships with opposing coaches and officials
- Make time for your family
- If you want to coach long term, you must have a supportive spouse
- Have a "date night" set aside every week for you and your spouse
- Include the other coach's wives
- Never stop learning. Always seek ways to improve
- Have fun!

If all you teach them is how to block, tackle, run, throw and catch… you've wasted a great opportunity! It is extremely important to build relationships with players, parents, coaching staff and their wives, administration, secretarial staff, custodial staff, teaching staff, community, area coaches and college coaches.

As a head coach, you must be prepared and have a plan for the following:

- Base offensive plays by down and distance
- Base defensive calls by down and distance
- Special teams
- Hurry field goal, onside kick, punt block and other special calls
- Substitutions
- Two minute drill
- Two point plays
- Trick plays
- Sideline and press box organization
- Pre game organization
- Halftime organization

- Post game organization
- Travel organization
- Detailed practice plans
- Scout teams
- Equipment
- Trainers
- Important summer dates sheet handed out before school gets out

You must not only be organized, but have a plan for everything you do. Every minute of practice is precious and must be utilized to its fullest. Don't waste time. Every drill, individual period, group period, special team period and team period, must have a purpose and relate directly to the game. For example, one thing I would do during our group pass period is have two receivers run a combination route and I would be the defender that the quarterback would read. I might be the flat defender, safety, corner, etc. We would have quarterbacks and receivers rotating one after the other to get as many reps in as possible. If we had enough players, we would do the same drill on the opposite side while another coach would be the read.

There was not one part of practice that did not have a purpose. Even after practice, when I addressed the team, there was a plan. I would always have the players take a knee. We did not have some standing, some sitting or some on two knees. Every player, unless injured, was on one knee. My reasoning was behind this was that first, it taught them discipline. Second, we did it together as a team. Third, it was easy for me to make eye contact with every player. I asked them to not look down, not look up, but look me in the eye so I know they were listening to what I was saying. Another example was that when addressing the team, I always faced the sun. By not having the sun in their eyes, they could easily focus on me. These may all seem like little things, but having a plan and a purpose, is extremely important.

During our team period, we never just ran plays from the same spot in the middle of the field. That was not realistic to what happens in the game, so why would we do it in practice. In fact, statistics show that 75% of plays in a game are from the hash marks, not in the middle of the field. As a result, I would script all our our plays so we would rotate where the ball was being snapped. We would start on the left hash and each play move across the field to the right, snapping the ball in one of five locations. Then, we would work our way back across the field from right to left. The snap locations we used were left hash, left middle, middle of field, right middle and right hash. Script the plays you want to run during your team period on your practice plan. Also next to the play, script what hash mark you are snapping the ball from. That way it's all built in to your practice plan in advance so you don't have to think about it during practice. It's a great utilization of time.

We always practiced "The Two Minute Drill" to prepare for the last two minutes of the game with no time outs. We always prepared the plays in advance. Our players knew that these were the plays that we would use in a game situation. We would start on our own 30 yard line while I signaled the plays. To stop the clock, we would try to get out of bounds or spike the ball. We would end the drill with a last second field goal as the clock was winding down. With about ten seconds left, I would yell, "hurry field goal" and begin counting down the seconds as our field goal team rushed onto the field. We practiced kicking the game winning field goal as the time expired. Then, the whole team would rush the field to congratulate our kicker, just as they would in a real game situation. This was always a great way to end practice. It was creating a critical game type situation, it was fun and built team camaraderie.

When practicing our goal line offense, we would place the ball on the ten yard line with four plays to score or we would lose the game. Again, the plays were always scripted in advance. Our players knew every week what plays we would be running in that goal line situation. The player that scored was instructed to run over to the Back Judge, who was always behind the defense, and hand him the ball. I always wanted our players to be respectful of the referees, so instead of just leaving the ball on the turf or some type of celebration, we always handed the ball to the official. I would have one of our assistants be designated as the Back Judge so everyone on our offense knew who to hand the ball to. It did not matter if all eleven of the defenders were on top of our player that scored. He was instructed to get up and run the ball over to the Back Judge. I felt that this showed discipline and class.

Another part of practice that needs careful planning includes individual drill work. I always tried to get as many players involved in the drill as possible. The fewer players that are standing around watching, the better. If only one player is involved in a drill while everyone else watches, the drill is a huge waste of time. For example, if I was coaching the offensive line on blocking technique and fundamentals, I would have everyone pair up with a partner across from each other on opposite sides of a white yard line. On my command, half of the players would be executing the same blocking technique with the partner across from them. After a few repetitions, they would switch roles with their partner. There are many ways to get several players involved in a drill at the same time regardless of a players position. The objective is to get as many repetitions for as many players as possible in the limited time you have available. Be organized. Have a plan and a purpose for everything you do. Don't waste time. Utilize every minute.

On public opinion:

"As an NFL coach, I received performance evaluations every day from multitudes of people, many of whom were completely unqualified to offer a valid critique"
Tony Dungy, *(former Indianapolis Colts coach)*

"99% of the fans don't know enough football to offer helpful advice. Fans only get to watch players on game day. We see them every day in practice. Fans do not watch game film to determine the best schemes for attacking an opponent"
Bobby Bowden, *(former FSU coach)*

"The coaching profession is very unstable. If you win enough games, you are often perceived as better than you really are. If you lose enough, you are sometimes treated as though you are inferior and incompetent. Usually, the truth lies somewhere in the middle"
Tom Osborn, *(former Nebraska coach)*

Advice to players

- Be committed
- Be a team player
- Be positive
- Show sportsmanship at all times
- Give your best effort at all times
- Listen to your coaches
- Any questions or complaints, talk to your coaches, not your parents
- Must be passionate about playing football
- Play football because you love it, not because of someone else
- Play for the fun of it
- Play other sports, so as to keep your competitive edge, not focusing on just one sport, while having fun enjoying high school

Advice for parents

- Support and encourage your kids
- Support the coaches in front of your kids
- Have your kids play because they want to, not because you want them to
- Don't discuss playing time or other athletes
- Go to the head coach first with any complaints, never above them
- If you're upset about something, wait 24 hours
- Be willing to help the program out without expecting anything in return
- Let the coaches coach. That's their job. That's what they're hired for

Every year at our "Meet The Team" night, I would tell the parents not to interfere with us coaches doing our job. "I would never think of going into your place of work and telling you how to do your job. Please don't tell me how to do mine!"

Advice for coaches families

- Wives support your husband. He's gone a lot, doing a job he loves, with great opportunities to have a positive impact on young people
- Encourage quality family time and date night during the week
- Ignore the negative fans. They will always be there, win or lose. Sit apart from them if possible

Advice for administrators

- Support your coach
- Be honest with your coach
- Communicate with your coach. Keep them informed of any issues so as not to be blindsided by it later
- Let the coaches coach. That's why you hired them
- Look for positives. Let the coaches know when they are doing a good job. Everyone works better with encouragement
- Do not discuss coaching with parents
- Socialize with your coaches. Maintain a friendship both in and out of school
- Go to games. Show your support
- Send all complaints through the proper channels… head coach, then to athletic director, then to administration

CHAPTER 10

FAVORITE QUOTES

"Failure to prepare certainly means preparing to fail."
John Wooden, *(former UCLA basketball coach)*

"Most battles are won even before they are fought."
General George Patton, WWII veteran

"Great games generally aren't a by product of inspirational speeches. Usually, they're by products of a great week of practice."
Mike Leach, *(former Texas Tech coach)*

"Pressure comes when someone calls on you to perform a task for which you are unprepared."
Tony LaRussa, *(former Oakland A's Manager)*

"Do it right, do it hard or do it again."
Bobby Bowden, *(former FSU coach)*

"There is no magic touch. Hard work, discipline and perseverance win more often than they lose."
Lou Holtz, (former Notre Dame coach)

"Don't have too many rules. Have as few as you possibly can, but enforce them."

Bobby Bowden, *(former FSU football coach)*

"A coach needs to be the most demanding when his team is doing well, because there's a human tendency to ease up when you're winning. When things go poorly, especially when the effort is there, that's when a team needs encouragement more than pressure from the coach."

Tom Landry, *(former Dallas Cowboys coach)*

"It's not the X's and the O's, it's the Jimmies and the Joes."

Jerry Kill, *(former University of Minnesota coach)*

"Coach a boy as if he were your own son."

Eddie Robinson, *(former Grambling coach)*

"You win with good people. Character is just as important as ability."

Don Shula, *(former Miami Dolphins coach)*

"Be more concerned with your character than your reputation, because your character is what you really are, while your reputation is merely what others think you are."

John Wooden, *(former UCLA basketball coach)*

"Don't let an undependable guy play just because he has great ability. He will let you down at a critical moment."

Bobby Bowden, *(former FSU football coach)*

"It's the nature of man to rise to greatness, if greatness is expected of him"

John Steinbeck, (Nobel Prize winning author)

"The key is not what you do, but who you are."

Tony Dungy, *(former Indianapolis Colts coach)*

"Twenty years from now you will be more disappointed by the things you didn't do than by the ones you did do. So throw off the bowlines, sail away from the safe harbor and catch the trade-winds in your sails. Explore. Dream. Discover."

Mark Twain

"Discipline is not what you do to someone, discipline is what you do for someone."

Lou Holtz, *(former Notre Dame coach)*

"Every man dies but not every man lives."

The movie *Braveheart*

"I wasn't called upon to succeed, I was called upon to try."

Mother Teresa

"Society places value on objects, wealth, size of our house and number of cars in our garage. Society emphasizes things like resumes, trophies, awards and winning. People are often assessed in the world by the things they acquire and so our calendars are often empty of time with our family. But whom will you call to your bedside in the last hours of life…your banker or stockbroker or your loved ones?"

Tony Dungy, *(former Indianapolis Colts coach)*

"So many coaches and players think they'll be satisfied if they win enough games or championships. However, the real secret of enjoying sports is to focus more on the process that the scoreboard,"

Tom Osborn, *(former Nebraska coach)*

CHAPTER 11

GRAYLING

1991

My first head coaching job was in Grayling, Michigan. Grayling is a small resort town. It is a great area for hunting, fishing, canoeing, golfing and snowmobiling. The high school enrollment was about 500 students. My first season coaching, we only had ten returning players. The entire backfield consisted of juniors who had played on the JV team the year before. All three of them were under 5'9" and under 160 pounds. Quite undersized for one player in the offensive backfield, let alone all three. One of my assistants was Don Ferguson who had been coaching for 34 years and was the head wrestling coach. The other assistant coach was Mike Branch who had been coaching for 27 years and was the athletic director. Mike's son, Steve, was a junior tight end and linebacker on the team. Both Don and Mike were great guys, fun to work with and great with the players.

My first game as a head football coach we lost to Roscommon 24-16 in triple overtime! After this game is when I realized how tough it could be coaching high school football. I had hopes of winning my first game ever as a head coach, especially after all the hard work we put in. It was depressing. I didn't like that feeling at all. I second guessed myself wondering what could I have done differently. After losing our second game, we won the next five straight games and went on to win the

Great Northern Conference Championship. This was the first outright championship for Grayling football in 20 years.

Along the way, we won a game 16-15 on a last second 40 yard field goal by Johannes Blekeli, who was a foreign exchange student from Norway after being down 15-0 at halftime. Johannes had never kicked a football prior to this season. He had played soccer back in Norway. I explained to him that his job would be to kick the ball between the goal posts, which would give us one point for an extra point or three points for a field goal. When he first started, he was aiming right in the middle of the uprights, but the ball naturally hooked and the ball continued to sail to the left. With the whole team watching, after a few missed attempts, I told him to start aiming for the right upright on the goal post, not down the middle. His next kick was going toward the right upright and then hooked perfectly to the left, right down the middle. The players all applauded. I then said to the entire team, "Now that's coaching!" everyone laughed as we ended practice. The following week we played at Onaway and won 24-0 to clinch the championship.

I instituted a couple of weekly awards that the players really liked. One was called "The Big Stick Award", which went to the player with the best hit of the game. I painted a 4"x4" piece of wood white with green letters. It had the name of the award, the players name, the opponent and the date. Another weekly award was called "The Pancake Award", which went to an offensive or defensive lineman that totally dominated the player over them. Since the linemen were in such close proximity, their chances of getting the Big Stick Award, was very slim, so I created this award. I painted the inside of a frying pan white with green letters. This award also had the name of the award, the players name, the opponent and the date.

1992

We had our starting backfield returning from a great year of experience. Along with the backfield, some other key players returned as well. As a team, we felt confident about the upcoming season and talked about winning another conference championship. Our players worked very hard in the off season and showed great team unity. Our motto for the season was "We Believe". In our opening game, we got revenge from our triple overtime loss to Roscommon the year before and beat them 41-14. We started the season 8-0 and won our second Great Northern Conference Championship in a row. However, we lost our final non-conference game of the regular season to Gaylord, before qualifying for the state playoffs.

In the fifth game of the season against Lincoln-Alcona, I told the players that it would be a tough game and that we could not win the championship without beating this team. I emphasized that this was the biggest game of the year. I knew if we beat them, we would have a great chance at winning the championship. Prior to the game, I gave every player and coach a t-shirt that said simply, "I Believe". I asked every player to put it on under their shoulder pads and to play with passion for four quarters. I told them that when the game is over, take your pads off and show our fans that we all believe in this team. That was exactly what happened. Parents were taking pictures as our players celebrated the 36-30 win, while proudly showing off their new sweaty t-shirts. After our next week win over Rogers City 28-6, we were ranked 7th in the state. The following week was our last conference game versus Whittemore-Prescott in blowing snow and freezing temperatures. The game was played at our home field. There was no way we were going to lose that game. Our players were very focused and determined to win. We dominated from the beginning, winning 53-6 and won our second straight conference championship.

After being 8-0, the mother of one of my players wrote a letter to the editor about what a bad coach I was. I was shocked! I thought to myself, how could she think that after what a great season have had. Her son was a great kid and he was a back up. She was upset that he did not play more in the games. Her son was very embarrassed about it and apologized to me, saying he had nothing to do with it and loved being part of the team. This was the first time as a head coach that I realized I am not going to please everyone. I quickly found out that it would not be the last complaint from a parent. Complaining from parents is part of the job. Sometimes, you just have to consider the source.

Our captains that year were great leaders. Gary Schroyer played running back and linebacker at 5'8" and 155 pounds. He rushed for over 1300 yards and was the Player of the Year in Northern Michigan. Mike Kirmo was our quarterback. He passed for almost 1300 yards and rushed for over 1000 yards. Steve Branch played tight end and linebacker, scoring

9 touchdowns on offense and was a leading tackler on defense. It was a great season. The players, parents, and fans were awesome. This was a season we will all remember for the rest of our lives.

1993

After graduating 22 seniors on the team the year before and returning only six juniors, we knew it could be a very difficult year. Also, the JV team last year was 0-9. We finished with a 2-7 record. Three of the losses were by an average of 2 points. The team consisted of a great group of guys to work with. They all had a great work ethic and never gave up. It was my first lesson in realizing that giving your best effort is all you can do. Regardless of coaching, schemes, and motivation, sometimes the opponent is just better than you. A key player for us was Chris Wolcott. He was the starting quarterback and free safety. His dad, Fred was one of my JV coaches and was a great friend.

I loved living in Grayling. I loved the players, the parents and the community, but when I got the phone call from Ralph Baldini, the principal at Flint Carman-Ainsworth, asking me to be the next head coach there, I had to say yes, it was a great opportunity. It was tough to leave, but I looked forward to the challenge that lay ahead.

CHAPTER 12

FLINT CARMAN-AINSWORTH

1994

I was excited about the opportunity to come back to Carman-Ainsworth, this time as the head coach instead of an assistant and getting my high school math position back. It was not going to be easy as I inherited a program that averaged just two wins in the past seven years. The school also finished in last place in the conference the year before and had not had a winning record in seven years (which was when I was an assistant). Coming back, I knew how tough the 'Big 9' Conference was in football. I had been an assistant coach at two of the conference's schools, Carman-Ainsworth for two years and Powers Catholic for two years. I also knew that Carman-Ainsworth did not have a good reputation as a football school. They were viewed as talented but undisciplined. Every school in the area wanted to schedule them. Many players on the team just wanted to wear the jersey around town but had a poor work ethic. The players were allowed to miss practice and still play in the game and football just simply was not high on their priority list. I knew that if our staff set high expectations, demanded discipline, hard work and teamwork, that we could turn the program around.

The local paper, 'The Flint Journal', conducted several interviews with me early-on in the season because I was the new guy taking over the losing program. One of my quotes they printed was, "There's no tradition; let's establish one". Another quote in the article said, "It's not going to be easy, but the way I look at it, the only way to go is up". I wanted to change as much as I possibly could about the way the team had approached things in the past. I wanted everyone to know that the team and the overall program was going to be far different. I changed the helmet logo, I got new uniforms and practiced on a different field than they had in the past. The players knew that things were changing for the better. They had about 60 players on the team the year before. We had about 35 for our first game because some guys just did not want to sacrifice enough to be part of the team. I told the team that it was not going to be easy, much more will be expected of them than previous years, but that it would all be worth it if they stay and be part of this turnaround. My two assistants were both former players in the program and ended up being two of my best friends. Jerry Parker and Rick Standen had both been All Conference players and were excellent coaches. Jerry was our defensive coordinator and Rick coached both the offensive and defensive line. I had actually coached Rick when I was an assistant at Carman-Ainsworth six years earlier. We had a new offense, defense, uniforms and attitude. I did everything that I could to make changes from what they had done last year. I had the players wear a sport coat, shirt and tie for their head and shoulder shots in the program. The week before our first game, the paper published another quote of mine that said, "How good we'll be, I don't know, but I do know we're going to go out there and get after it. This will be a much different team than people have seen in the past".

In our first game, we beat Flint Beecher 40-14, who Carman-Ainsworth had never beat before. Flint Beecher has produced many great college and pro players. The headlines in The Flint Journal Sports section read, "Cavaliers Beat Bucs For First Time Ever". After starting 3-0 and everyone excited, we played Powers Catholic where I was an assistant for two years under Bill Tucker before taking my first head coaching job in Grayling. It was a packed house and a great game. Unfortunately, we lost 12-14. Powers Catholic was a strong team that year and we had only lost by two. This game sent the message to every other team in the conference that Carman-Ainsworth had definitely improved. We finished that first season 6-3 and the community was fired up about the football team again. More importantly, our players that bought-in to our new approach were proud to be Carman-Ainsworth football players and were excited about the future. I made the comment that even though our community was thrilled with our 6-3 record, that it was a good start, but I had much larger goals for this program.

1995

With only eight returning starters, three on offense and five on defense, most coaches would not be very optimistic about the upcoming season. After that first season of 6-3, with me as their new coach, our players were developing confidence. Two of our key returners were named James Willingham, who was a running back/defensive back and Ryan Sergent, who was a tight end/linebacker. In the first game against Flint Beecher (which we won 32-13) James Willingham rushed only 8 times for 154 yards. Nearly 20 yards per carry! He was having a great game until he tore his ACL and would miss his entire senior year. It was a devastating loss for all of us, especially James. He was a gifted athlete who had been recruited by several Division 1 schools. The following week, we beat Flushing 29-14. Jermarx Marsh, who filled in for James, averaged over six yards per carry. In our third game, we beat Swartz Creek 54-6. Our sophomore quarterback, Brian Delorge, passed the ball for 3 touchdowns and ran in for two more. In addition, Jermarx Marsh stepped up again rushing for 160 yards on 12 carries, averaging about 13.5 yards per carry.

After our first three games, we had outscored our opponents 103-14. I was so proud of what this team had accomplished so far. Especially since the previous two seasons before I became the head coach, they had only won one game in one of those seasons and two in another. We had a huge game in week 4 at Powers Catholic, who was always one of the best teams in the conference. We beat our rival and my good friend, head coach Bill Tucker, 29-28 in overtime to continue the winning season 4-0. This was an outstanding win for our program! The Flint Journal headline read, "There Can Be No Doubt Now, Carman-Ainsworth Is For Real". We finished the season 7-2, one win more than the first year and qualified for the state playoffs.

Jermarx Marsh was named 1st team All-Conference and got a scholarship to Grand Valley State University after coming off the bench in game one when James Willingham tore his ACL. James got a full ride scholarship to Eastern Michigan University, the only Division 1 school that honored his scholarship. Ryan Sergent, our starting tight end/linebacker, had a great year and showed excellent leadership. Ryan went on to a great career as a tight end at Albion College. Brian Delorge, our sophomore quarterback, showed great promise and was named 2nd Team All-Conference. It was comforting knowing we had him coming back for two more years!

1996

My third year, the returners were junior, Brian Delorge, quarterback and junior Jim Delbridge, who anchored both the offensive and defensive lines. Only four returning starters on offense and four on defense. We brought Mike Delorge, Brian's younger brother, up to varsity to be our starting center and the defensive lineman. He was only a freshman. I had never before had a freshman as a starter on varsity, but Mike was physically and mentally up for the challenge. Two other newcomers to varsity were our running backs, Calvin Sims and Derek Dantzler. Calvin was bigger guy at about 6'3" and 200 pounds, while Derek was smaller at about 5'9" and 165 pounds. Both would be great running backs for us for the next two years. I had implemented the Split Back Veer Offense after taking over the Carman-Ainsworth job thinking that running triple option football would give our guys a good chance to compete. In doing so, our quarterback was just as much a threat to run the ball as our running backs were and Brian Delorge was the perfect triple option quarterback. He was smart, fast and tough.

We opened the season with a 41-0 win over Flint Beecher and had 256 yards of total offense. In our fourth game against Owosso, we won 41-20 and all three of our backs had two rushing touchdowns. Delorge, the quarterback, scored from 30 and 64 yards out and had two 2-point conversions. Sims, one of our running backs, scored from 39 and 40 yards out and Dantzler, the other running back, scored from 19 and 59 yards out. We beat Grand Blanc the next week in a close one, 21-20. Delorge rushed for 183 yards for two touchdowns. In week six, we beat Flushing 45-21 with Delorge rushing for 177 yards and scored three touchdowns.

Unfortunately Brian broke his leg in that game and would be out for the season. We were 5-1 at the time and finished the season 6-3. When Brian broke his leg, I felt terrible for him and the rest of the team because he was such an integral part of our success. Brian had worked extremely hard and was having great season as our quarterback. Fortunately, Brian was only a junior and would return as our starting quarterback for his senior year

1997

We felt confident returning our entire backfield along with some key linemen on offense. Overall, we had nine returning starters on offense and five on defense. Having Brian Delorge back as a three-year starter at quarterback was a huge advantage along with two-year starters at running back, Calvin Sims and Derek Dantzler.

We started the season 3-0, averaging over 43 points per game. I was optimistic about this season, especially with the senior class we had. I felt very proud of the job our coaches and players had done over the last few years since I became the head coach at Carman-Ainsworth. They continued to buy in to way of doing things and it was paying off. We lost in week four to a very good Ann Arbor Huron team in a non conference game, then bounced back to win four of our next five games, finishing 7-2. In our seventh game, we played Grand Blanc, which was always a really good game against a tough team. We won another close one, 35-33 and the hero of the game was a tiny 5'5", 120 pound wide receiver named Tony Beauchamp. Tony had three catches for 101 yards and two touchdowns. As the unexpected star of the game, Tony was hugged by his teammates, coaches and fans. Another great lesson in football that you never know when it will be your turn to step up and make big plays for your team, so you must be ready for that moment. Seniors Brian Delorge at quarterback, Calvin Sims at running back, and Jim Delbridge at offensive tackle, were named 1st team All Conference, along with Sophomore Mike Delorge at center. Brian Delorge had 849 yards rushing, which was the most in Big 9 Conference history in 1997. He also scored 17 touchdowns his senior year. Brian and Derek Dantzler both received scholarships to play at Saginaw Valley State University. Calvin Sims was now 6'4" and 210 pounds. We used him as both a running back and wide receiver. Calvin was highly recruited and accepted a scholarship to play at Michigan State University. He eventually transferred to Southern Illinois University to finish his career. Jim Delbridge our 6'5" 250 pound offensive tackle got a scholarship to play at the Air Force Academy.

1998

After four years of coaching at Carman-Ainsworth, we felt that our players had taken great pride in their effort, were very confident and believed in our system. Each year, our teams worked hard, showed great discipline and were committed. With only three returning starters on offense and four on defense, we were very inexperienced. Two senior transfers helped in that area. Brent Rogers was a big running back/linebacker and Garvin Ringwelski was a very talented kicker and punter. After the season, Rogers earned a scholarship to Saginaw Valley State University and Ringwelski earned one to Temple University. We lost our opening game by one point, then won our next two conference games. In the third game, we beat Flushing, who were the defending Big 9 Conference champs, 55-38. We lost to Ann Arbor Huron again the next week, in our only non conference game. We then won our last five games averaging over 49 points per game. In our last game versus Swartz Creek, we won 62-14 and our junior running back, Kenyun Pittman, scored five touchdowns to tie the Big 9 record. We finished the season 7-2 and were optimistic about the experience we had coming back next year. In addition to Rogers and Ringwelski making 1st Team All Conference, three juniors did also. Mike Delorge, who was a 3 year starter and was 1st team on both offense and defense. Jason Shaheen, offensive tackle and Brian Cook, linebacker were the other two juniors.

1999

Even with the success we previously had the past five seasons, we felt that this was our best team yet and our opponents knew it. We were picked as the conference favorite and the Flint Journal headline read, "Word on the Cavs is they're loaded". In our opener, we defeated the conference champ from last season, Kearsley, 41-10. That game got everyone's attention. Our quarterback, Tony Carr, rushed for 192 yards on 16 carries, which was two yards shy of Brian Delorge's Big 9 Conference record. Tony was a great athlete and also started at corner. He ended up getting a scholarship to play at Western Michigan University. We beat Davison in week 2, 49-28 and Flushing in week 3, 36-15. Going into the Flushing game, we were averaging 45 points a game and they were averaging 43 points a game. We played at Flushing and without our starting running back, Kenyun Pittman, who had a foot injury. In that game, we set a Big 9 Conference record by rushing for 522 yards. We had three 100 yard rushers in that game. Tony Carr, our quarterback, had 183 yards. Aaron Mundale, our running back, had 135 yards and scored three touchdowns. The surprise of the game was David Vennie, who started in place of Kenyun and rushed for 204 yards and scored a touchdown. In week four, we got our first win versus Ann Arbor Huron in three years, by the score of 55-36. Our defense held them to 46 yards rushing and Tony Carr scored three touchdowns while rushing for 157 yards. Next up was Powers Catholic, which was always a tough game. This time their long time head coach, Bill Tucker, was on our sidelines as an assistant coaching against his former team. We beat Powers 17-10 to improve to 5-0. Our defense again stepped up, holding them to only 53 yards rushing. We beat Flint Beecher the next week 54-0 behind Aaron Mundale's three rushing touchdowns. Our next game against Clio, we won 56-6. Both of our running backs had a great game. Kenyun Pittman rushed for 173 yards and scored two touchdowns. Aaron Mundale rushed for 132 yards and scored two touchdowns as well. It was Aaron's 16th touchdown of the season and he led the entire Flint area in scoring.

Week eight was the game everyone anticipated. It was for the conference championship at Grand Blanc. Both teams were 7-0. They had a great running back named Reggie Benton, who was the all time career rushing leader in Genesee county and going to play at the University of Michigan next fall. We won the game 28-27 in front of the largest crowd in the history of Genesee county football to date, the record still stands. It was one of the most amazing games I had ever been part of. The hype going into the game from the fans and press was amazing. The size of the crowd was unlike anyone had seen or played in front of. When we took the field to start the game, it was like a parting of the seas just getting from our locker room to the field. I had chills running down my spine and wasn't even playing. I just hoped that our players would be able to channel all that excitement into great execution of our offense, defense and special teams. These were the two best teams in the conference, both undefeated, in a frenzied atmosphere, playing for the championship. Carman-Ainsworth had never won the Big 9 Conference Championship until that day. We held their star running back to only 60 yards rushing, while our running back, Kenyun Pittman, rushed for 187 yards and scored two touchdowns. Two big plays sealed the win for us. Tony Carr, who had two interceptions in the game, knocked down a two point conversion pass and we blocked a long, last-second field goal. It was pandemonium after that win. Our fans rushed the field. All of our players and coaches were celebrating this milestone win with the thousands of parents, friends and fans that attended.

We finished the regular season with a perfect 9-0 record and the school's first ever Big 9 Conference Championship! I had planted the seed all week about how awesome it will be to win this game. Before the game, I had the players visualize winning the game, our fans rushing the field to congratulate them, along with hugging their teammates, family and friends. I asked them to think about how great it will feel and that for the rest of your life, you can say that you were Big 9 Champs. I also told them that I was so confident we were going to win that I was having one of our managers video tape the entire night, from getting ready in our locker room, to the bus ride there, pregame warm ups, sideline shots during the game and the celebration on the field afterwards. Every player would get a copy to vividly remember the excitement of that night.

We still had one more conference game to play and that was at Swartz Creek. The coaching staff emphasized all week that we did not want to be "Co-Champs", we wanted to win it outright, which we would accomplish with a win. Our guys played with great passion and pride, winning 41-0. We lost in the second round of the playoffs that year. Tony Carr broke Brian Delorge's conference rushing record and was the first quarterback in Big 9 history to rush for over 1000 yards. He also had 12 touchdowns rushing.

We set some amazing records that year. We had eleven players make 1st Team All Conference, which is the most in the 39 year history of the Big 9 Conference. Mike Delorge, at 6'0" 240, was 1st Team on both offense and defense for the third year in a row. He was also named 'All State'. Tony Carr made 1ˢᵗ Team both ways also as quarterback and defensive back. Both of our running backs, Kenyun Pittman and Aaron Mundale, made 1ˢᵗ Team. It was only the second time in Big 9 history that two running backs from the same team both rushed for over 1000 yards. Mundale scored 17 touchdowns and was the second leading scorer in the conference. Pittman averaged 13 yards per carry, which led the conference. We had three offensive linemen make 1ˢᵗ Team; Delorge, Jason Shaheen and Mike Newton. Defensively, we were led by 1ˢᵗ Team linebacker, Brian Cook, who was a two-year starter. Brian had set a school and conference record with 111 tackles. In addition to these, we had two other 1ˢᵗ Team selections with defensive lineman Antwan Johnson and linebacker, Landon Kelly. In our eight conference games that year, we averaged over 40 points per game and held our opponents to 12 points per game.

CHAPTER 13

JENISON

2000

After the complete turnaround at Flint Carman-Ainsworth and coming off that 9-0 season, winning the first ever conference championship, I never thought I would leave. I was coaching in the area that I grew up as a kid and had the program heading in the right direction.

Jenison's athletic director, Kevin VanDyn, had been calling me, saying that they wanted me to be their next football coach after a good friend of mine, Tony Annese, had just resigned to become the head coach at Muskegon High School. I was flattered they offered, but really not interested at the time. As they persisted, I thought if I made one more move as a head coach, the west side of Michigan would be a place I would like to live and raise my family. I finally said yes and accepted the position as the head football coach at Jenison High School. I also looked forward to the challenge of playing in the OK Red Conference, which is one of the toughest in the state. Unlike Carman-Ainsworth, Jenison had been successful under Annese and before him, Dave Woodcock, both of whom were good friends of mine. Because there was already a winning tradition there, I decided to keep the uniforms the same as they had been for several years. Although Tony had encouraged me to take the job, he did tell me that most of the teams in this conference will have better talent than you, but the kids will work hard and I think you'll like it here. In addition, they had just passed a bond issue to do a complete renovation of the football stadium with new artificial turf, seating, press box, locker rooms, entryway and more.

My wife, Terry and I along with our three kids moved into a brand new home in Jenison and looked forward to the opportunities of living in West Michigan. My oldest daughter, Laura was going into her sophomore year and would have me as her Geometry teacher. Lyndsay, our middle child, was only five and Luke, our youngest was only three. In our first game, we beat Grand Rapids Catholic Central 20-14, but lost our second game to neighboring rival, Hudsonville by one point, 27-28. That would be our only loss of the regular season, finishing 8-1. In week four, we beat perennial power Rockford 42-21, which shocked everyone. I told our players that in the first three games we had not played a good, solid, total game yet. I asked the players before the game to commit to playing a solid four quarters of football. They did. Every player on the team played their hearts out. We scored on six of our first eight possessions. In one of the most memorable plays of the season, on 4th and short from midfield, I decided to go for it. We had been primarily a running team at that point and Rockford knew it. Expecting them to pack the line of scrimmage, I called for a play action "dump" pass from our junior quarterback, Jeremy Landstra, to our junior tight end, Joe Diekevers. I felt it could be wide open for the first down and if it worked, would give us the momentum to finish the game with tremendous confidence. Not only did we get the first down, Joe ran untouched for the touchdown. The play worked to perfection. The entire defense bit on the run fake and Joe was wide open. Our home crowd fans were shocked at the call and went crazy as Joe ran across the goal line. Landstra was starting his first game of the season at quarterback in place of Austin Amato, who was an excellent all around player that we wanted to move around and get him the ball in different ways. Amato ended up with 126 yards rushing and two touchdowns. Mike DeHaan, the other running back, had 136 yards and two touchdowns. Landstra had 140 yards passing and two touchdowns. He also ran for 80 yards. The headlines in the Grand Rapids Press newspaper the next morning was, "Playing their hearts out, Jenison topples rival Rockford".

Our next game against Holland West Ottawa, we won 10-6 on a sloppy field after a lightning delay in the first quarter. We were down 3-6, had a 70 yard, 13 play drive and quarterback Jeremy Landstra avoiding a sack, with a defender hanging on him, threw a 5 yard touchdown strike to Joe Diekevers with one second left to win the game.

The following week, we beat Holland 32-12 with five different players scoring. Landstra threw a 20 yard touchdown pass to Joe Diekevers and ran one in from 37 yards out. After twisting his ankle in the second quarter, Landstra was replaced by Austin Amato who threw a 52 yard touchdown pass to Charlie Hall. Mike DeHaan had 105 yards rushing and one touchdown. Aaron Dawkins scored on a five yard run.

In week seven, we beat Grand Haven 20-13 behind Jeremy Landstra's 127 yards passing and a 35 yard touchdown pass to Charlie Hall. Austin Amato had 113 yards rushing and a 15 yard touchdown run.

We beat East Kentwood in week nine to win the OK Red Conference Championship 35-14 and qualified for the state playoffs. We did not have any outstanding athletes on that team, but a great group of hard working, team players. It was an interesting season with many key contributors to our success. We only lost one game and that was by a single point.

As we were preparing to face Grand Rapids Creston in the first round of the state playoffs, I was injured and hospitalized in a freak accident in practice the day before the game. I was the scout team quarterback and on a play action run fake to sophomore Bruce Harder, his left elbow caught me right in the throat as he formed a pocket with his arms. I dropped to the ground and could not breathe. The whole team and staff were shocked and not sure what had happened. When I did stand, I could not talk and was very sore. Nobody felt worse than Bruce Harder thinking that his first week practicing with the varsity, he knocked the head coach out the day before the playoff game. After going to the hospital after practice, they wanted me to stay overnight, which I objected to since our game was the next day. The hospital agreed to let me go home, but said I cannot teach on Friday and that no way should I coach in the game. After much rumbling at school about why the head coach was not there on game day, I announced to meet with the players immediately after school to let them know I was alright. I really was not alright. I could not even talk, I could barely whisper. Coaching from the sidelines and not being able to talk, let alone raise your voice so players can hear you on the field was so frustrating.

I had always been the scout team quarterback to prepare our defense each week. Having played quarterback in high school and college, I felt I could not only give our defense the best look possible, but also get the plays in and out quickly, keeping the scout team focused and excited about preparing our defense for the next opponent. We brought several sophomores up from the JV team for the playoffs and one of them, Bruce Harder, was playing running back. We ended up losing that playoff game, but looked back on a very memorable season.

During that championship season of 2000, one of our best athletes was our quarterback/defensive back, Austin Amato. Austin was small, but very quick and great at running our triple option. I felt that moving him around and getting the ball in his hands a variety of ways, was best for our team. Austin's back up was a junior, two year starter at outside linebacker, named Jeremy Landstra. Jeremy, who was also a great wrestler, was bigger, stronger and had a great arm. Midway through the season, we began playing Jeremy more at quarterback, where we could be effective both running the ball and passing, while we move Austin around and found different ways to get him the ball. I felt it was a good move for our team. With Jeremy returning for his senior year, along with a good group of receivers and not many running backs, it was necessary to look at changing our offense in the offseason to take advantage of the talent we had. It would prove to be one of the best coaching decisions I ever made.

2001

We only returned two offensive starters and three defensive starters from the championship team a year earlier. On offense, we only had quarterback Jeremy Landstra and offensive tackle Matt Bremer returning. Our junior class was coming off a 5-4 JV season. On paper we did not appear to have a great team. However, I knew that with the skilled players we had returning, that implementing the Spread Offense would give our team the best chance to be successful, along with some of the same option concepts we had used in the past. So, I spent quality time with some of the best college programs who ran the Spread very effectively. I visited Northwestern and Purdue during spring practices, watched a lot of video tape and spent quality time learning from their coaches. I also had a great resource only ten minutes away with Grand Valley State University and their coach, Brian Kelly. With all this information, I had to pair it down so it could be easy to implement and understand for our players. Another advantage was we were the first team in our area to run the spread, so our opponents would not be used to defending it. I read once that you should always be one of the first to implement a new concept, not one of the last.

Even though we lined up with four wide receivers and one running back most of the time, we were a very balanced offense between running and passing. With the passing concepts I had learned from the college coaches, and running a fast paced no huddle offense, we were able to keep the defense on their heels. Once again, we did not have great talent, but kids that bought in to the system, executed it and had fun. At 6'1 and 215 pounds, quarterback Jeremy Landstra was outstanding both running and throwing the ball. Our running back, Steve Elenbaas, also had a great year running the ball. Steve was only 5'8" and 170 pounds, but tough, strong and elusive.

In our opener, we beat Grand Rapids Catholic Central 37-16. Landstra completed 15/20 passes for 198 yards and two touchdowns. He also ran for one. Steve Elenbaas rushed 19 times for 134 yards and two touchdowns. Senior Joe Diekevers, had six catches for 60 yards and a touchdown. Junior Derek Nelson, had four catches for 75 yards and junior Drew Jenison, had three catches for 28 yards and one touchdown. Nelson was playing in his first football game ever after having been the goalie on the soccer team and would become a huge player for us over the next two seasons.

After winning our first two games of the season, we lost the next two by a total of four points. We won our next four games averaging over 45 points per game. In week eight, we beat East Kentwood in a shootout 47-36. Steve Elenbaas set a school record with 325 yards rushing on 40 carries. He also ran for four touchdowns. Jeremy Landstra completed 14/21 passes for 178 yards and two touchdowns to Derek Nelson and Joe Diekevers. We beat Grandville 35-20 in our last regular season game and finished 7-2, qualifying for the state playoffs again.

We beat Forest Hills Northern 31-7, in the first round of the playoffs, but then had to face a very talented Grand Rapids Creston team for the district championship the following Saturday afternoon. We played on a beautiful, sunny, fall afternoon on the artificial turf at Houseman Field in Grand Rapids, which was Creston's home field. Our staff knew this would be the best team we would play all year. They had seven Division 1 scholarship players on their team. We had none. I felt that our players were somewhat intimidated by Creston's size, speed and athleticism at first. I encouraged them to go out and execute our game plan and we would be fine. I told our team to give it all you got for one half and we would meet back here in the locker room to see where we were at. There were five different lead changes in the game and several big plays for both teams. With the superior talent they had, we had to play a great game to win. We had kept them off balance offensively, effectively mixing the run and the pass. Jeremy Landstra threw a pair of touchdown passes to Derek Nelson in the first quarter, one for 3 yards and the other for 71 yards. Steve Elenbaas scored on a 1 yard run late in the second quarter. We came in at halftime leading 21-9. I congratulated our team on keeping their composure and executing our game plan despite being quite nervous before the game. Now that we played one half of football and were in the lead, I challenged them to go out and play the second half with tremendous confidence that we would win this game. I reminded our players of the great feeling of accomplishment we'd have after we won. I expected our team to play even better in the second half and come out with a big win. They did. In the fourth quarter, Joe Diekevers 47 yard interception return set up a 17 yard touchdown run by Elenbaas. After a fumble recovery by our linebacker, J.J. Reed, Elenbaas scored on a 70 yard run. Derek Nelson made 3 of 4 extra point kicks and caught a two point conversion pass. We played with great confidence in the second half knowing we could beat this team and won 35-22. It was one of the greatest wins I have ever been a part of. On paper, we had no chance against this team, but that is why we play football, and that is what made it so special for our players and fans. Every time I see their coach, Sparky McEwen, he reminds me that I would never win a bigger game. Sparky went on to be the head coach of the Grand Rapids Rampage in the Arena League and is now head coach at Division 2, Davenport University.

We came home the next week to beat Saginaw Heritage 35-14 in the Regional Championship behind the passing of Jeremy Landstra. Landstra completed 33/47 passes for 355 yards and four touchdowns. In the first quarter, Landstra threw a 15 yard touchdown pass to Drew Jenison and

Steve Elenbaas scored on a 14 yard run. In the second quarter, Landstra threw a pair of touchdown passes, one to Derek Nelson for 9 yards and the other to Brady Wilson for 25 yards. That put us up 28-14 at halftime. Landstra threw a 3 yard touchdown pass in the fourth quarter to Eric Wierenga. Derek Nelson was 5 for 5 on extra point kicks. The win set us up for a Semi-Final game with Wyandotte Roosevelt at a neutral site in Lansing, Michigan with the winner moving on to the State Championship Game on Thanksgiving weekend. We beat Wyandotte 28-7 on a sunny November afternoon with another balanced attack of both running and passing. Our starting running back, Steve Elenbaas, was unable to play due to an ankle injury and Bruce Harder, now a junior, stepped up in his place and did a great job rushing for 119 yards on 13 carries. Gary Andrew opened the scoring with a 4 yard touchdown run in the first quarter, followed by Landstra's 13 yard touchdown run in the second, to put us ahead 14-0 at halftime. Landstra scored on a 20 yard run in the fourth quarter to put us up 21-7. Late in the fourth quarter, Landstra threw a 16 yard touchdown pass to Brady Wilson, who made a spectacular catch in the corner of the end zone to finish the scoring. Derek Nelson was 4 for 4 on extra point kicks. Brady Wilson finished with 6 catches for 70 yards and Jeremy Landstra was 15/22 for 179 yards passing.

Jenison High School was now playing in the State Championship Game for the first time in school history. We had won eleven games that year, which no Jenison team had ever done. It was an exciting week in school and at practice with the anticipation of the big game. Unfortunately, we lost the game to Chippewa Valley, but the experience our players and the thousands of Jenison fans had will forever be a great memory. Our only scores came in the 3rd quarter. Brady Wilson scored the first ever touchdown for Jenison High School in a state championship game on a 10 yard pass from Jeremy Landstra. A fumble recovery by Joe Diekevers set up a 7 yard touchdown run by Eric Wierenga. As hard as it was for our players to end their season with a loss in the championship game, I had to remind them of how fortunate they were to have even gone this far and how proud us coaches and the entire community were of what they had accomplished. I also mentioned that once you are in the playoffs, there is only one team that finishes the season with a win and that is the state champion. We were escorted back into Jension by police cars and fire trucks with their lights flashing and sirens blaring while our die-hard fans lined the streets. Everyone was so proud of our guys, especially me. We went directly to our gymnasium for a welcome back reception. It was packed! The outpouring of support for these young men who had such a great season was overwhelming. It was just what they needed after a tough loss and help put the whole season into perspective. One of the most memorable and rewarding football seasons I have ever had in my coaching career.

After this great season, our quarterback Jeremy Landstra, broke all of the Jenison High School passing records and went on to play at Grand Rapids Community College. Our running back Steve Elenbaas, broke the Jenison rushing record and walked on at Grand Valley State. We had three players go to Division III, Hope College, J.J. Reed, Brady Wilson and Joe Diekevers. J.J. was our starting linebacker, Brady was a starting wide receiver, and Joe started both ways as a receiver and outside linebacker. Brady and Joe went on to play for four years at Hope and Joe was named team captain his senior year.

Our team captains were chosen by the players prior to the season. The captains were linemen Matt Bremer at 6'4" 245 pounds and Brandon Branch at 5'9" and 225 pounds, defensive end Gary Andrew at 5'8" and 215 pounds and our quarterback Jeremy Landstra at 6'1" and 215 pounds.

There are two inspirational stories from this season that I want to share. One is about Dave Woodcock, a former head coach at Jenison and good friend of mine, who I convinced to come out of retirement and coach. The other, is about Gary Andrew, who came a long way to be our starting defensive end and team captain. Dave Woodcock had been the head coach at Jenison High School for many years. I had met "Woody", through the Michigan High School Football Coaches Association. He was a past president and I was a regional rep at the time. Dave came down with some type of neurological damage and could not walk right around the time I got the head coaching job at Jenison. He and his wife Parm, were living in a cottage on a lake about an hour away. Dave was in a wheelchair but the cottage was not handicap accessible. I remember picking him up at the cottage and taking him to an association meeting. He told me how depressing it was to sit in that wheelchair, looking out the window and how he always felt trapped. He told me that he felt like he was just waiting to die, and had nothing to live for. I encouraged him to move back to the Jenison area where he would be close to family and friends. I also told Dave that if he came back, I would like to have him coach with me. He needed something to live for and football had always been his passion. He did find a handicap accessible condo nearby and moved back prior to our 2001 season. That was a huge step for him, but the clincher would be his return to coaching. Dave coached our defensive line from a battery operated Amigo wheelchair. His seat would swivel so he could turn to one side and coach sitting down. Although he could not walk, Dave did a great job coaching from that wheelchair and quickly earned the respect of the players with his knowledge and passion for the game. One day at practice, he was barking out some instructions to his group and was so intent on getting his point across, that he stood up and took about four steps towards the players to emphasize a point. Knowing that he had not walked in over a year, the players and coaches were completely shocked to see him out of that wheelchair and walking. The entire practice stopped and everyone applauded at what they had just witnessed. Dave was just as shocked as the rest of us that he had stood up and walked! He continued to improve physically and soon was walking with just a cane. The doctors had no medical explanation for his rapid improvement. After the state championship game, with Coach Woodcock on the sidelines, the Grand Rapids Press had interviewed Dave about what it was like to be back coaching football again, especially after how far he had come since the nerve damage that put him in a wheelchair. He explained how much fun he had throughout the season working with the players and coaches. He also publicly thanked me for inviting him to come back and coach. He said, "I thank Coach Larkin for giving me the opportunity to coach again. He saved my life and gave me a reason to live".

Gary Andrew was a sophomore when we first met. I was touring Jenison High School when the athletic director introduced me to Gary, who played on the JV team earlier that year. Initially, he was not very friendly to me, in fact, seemed very indifferent. Gary was only 5"6", but a stocky, well built kid. I was informed that Gary was going through a very difficult time in his life because his mother had committed suicide a few years earlier and Gary was the one who found her. Gary did not have any relatives that could take him in. His biological father was not involved in

Gary's life. Gary went to live with a friend's family to start his freshman year, which was not a great environment for him and only perpetuated his problem. He needed to be in a much more stable environment because at the rate he was going, would never graduate, let alone be eligible to play football. Gary was a very angry and depressed young man since the death of his mother. With no family to fall back on and hold him accountable, he was not doing well in school. He was getting suspended quite often and his grades were bad. He simply didn't care. Out of school he wasn't making good decisions either. Gary's junior year was his first year playing varsity football and my first year as the head football coach at Jenison. He was suspended for the first two games his junior year and didn't participate in our summer workouts. I told Gary that he would be on the scout team during the suspension and that he would need to work so hard and with such a great attitude, that we'd have no choice but to start him in week three after coming off his suspension. I also told him that most importantly, he needed to prove to his teammates and coaches that we could all count on him based on his effort and attitude. To Gary's credit, he worked his tail off and did everything we asked of him. He was determined to show everyone how much he loved football and that he deserved to be a starter. We couldn't block him on the scout team. He was so dominate that he earned a starting spot at defensive end for the rest of his junior season and a key part of our conference championship team that year. Although things were improving in Gary's life both academically and in football, I knew that we had to do intervene and get him into a different home. We needed to keep him positive, and encourage him to continue to work hard or I was concerned he could slide backwards into his old ways. If I could not find a good home for Gary with one of his teammates, I was prepared to take him in myself.

Prior to Gary's senior year, I asked our starting wide receiver, Brady Wilson, if he would be willing to have Gary live with him and his family. I knew this would be a great fit for Gary and really help him get his life back on track. Brady agreed, then I talked to his parents, Brian and Shelly about it. After discussing it as a family, they agreed to take Gary in. From then on, Gary continued to improve in all aspects of his life. He worked hard in football and in school. His grades were going up, he didn't have any disciplinary issues and his teammates were so impressed with his work ethic that they voted Gary as one of the four team captains prior to his senior season. At only 5'6" and just over 200 pounds, Gary was our starting defensive end. Although he was undersized for that position, Gary played his heart out in every game and at every practice. His teachers were amazed at his transformation from a bitter, troubled kid that did not perform well in school, to a young man that was happy, confident and had his priorities in order. I was so proud of what Gary had accomplished. I was especially proud of him after having such a great senior season, being named team captain and starting his last game in the state championship game. Brian and Shelly Wilson took Gary in, treated him like their own son and had great influence in turning his life around.

I ran into Gary at church a couple years after he had graduated. I did not know he went to the same church I did. I did not even know what he had been doing since high school. Gary approached me with a big smile and gave me a huge hug. I immediately was reminded of this same gruff, troubled teenager when I had first met him his sophomore year and was still amazed at the change. When I asked what he was doing now, Gary told me how happy he was with his personal, professional and spiritual life. He was in a great relationship, had a good job that he liked and was doing some church ministry. I told him how happy I was for him and how great he looked. We both had tears in our eyes reminiscing his senior year. Then he said, "Coach Larkin, I can't thank you enough for believing in me. I wouldn't be here today if it wasn't for you". That makes coaching all worthwhile!

2002

We had five returning starters on offense and four on defense. Three of our offensive linemen were back. We had center Chris VanDalsen, guard Adam Rhoda, and tackle James Tanis. Two receivers were back including; Derek Nelson and Eric Wierenga. We moved Kyle Palmatier, who was a starting guard his junior year, to a wide receiver his senior year. Steve Brander would be the starting quarterback after backing up Jeremy Landstra his junior year. Steve was 6'4", over 200 pounds, athletic, and had a good arm. After opening the season with a 40-0 win over Grand Rapids Catholic Central and a 34-20 win over arch rival Hudsonville, we got a good beating by Holland West Ottawa 21-56. In our next three games, we averaged 45 points per game and were now 5-1. We would end up losing two of our last three games, finishing 6-3 and qualifying for the state playoffs. In our week eight win over Grandville 23-6, Brander threw for 168 yards and two touchdowns. In one game, Brander completed 41 passes, setting a new state record. In the first round of the state playoffs, we had to face West Ottawa again. After beating us by 35 points, in week three, we lost by only nine 33-42.

Steve Brander would go on to get a scholarship to Saginaw Valley State to play quarterback. After being a back up for two years, he switched to tight end and became a starter. Steve played at 6'4", 250 pounds and was one of the top tight ends in the GLIAC. Derek Nelson, a two year starter at wide receiver and former soccer goalie who did not play football until his junior year, got a scholarship to play at Hillsdale College. Chris VanDalsen, a two year starter at center got a scholarship to Grand Valley State.

2003

After losing most of our starters from the previous year, playing with a very inexperienced team and competing in the always tough OK Red Conference, we knew this season would be a great challenge. We did return two good athletes in Tony Clausen and Pete Trammell. Tony was only 5'9" and we used him as a receiver, quarterback and running back on offense, along with being a starting corner on defense. He was also our return man for kickoffs and punts. Pete Trammell was a 6'4" wide receiver and defensive back. He was a starter on the basketball team as well and probably their best player.

We opened the season with a close win over Grand Rapids Catholic Central 13-12, for the fourth time in a row. We gave up 69 points the following week to a very explosive East Kentwood team resulting in a loss. In week three, we lost a close one to West Ottawa 20-27. We beat Forest Hills Northern in our fourth game 33-13, putting us at 2-2 on the season and facing our neighbor rivals, Hudsonville, who were 4-0. Our guys played a great game and we came out with a big win, 35-27. We played Rockford the following week, who was always at the top of the conference and always seems loaded with talented players. We lost 24-27, but our players gave it their all. We won two out of our last three games, averaging 40 points a game in our two wins. In our last regular season game, we beat Muskegon Reeths-Puffer with a score of 39-14. Our quarterback, B.J. Wells had great game completing 21/30 passes for 293 yards and three touchdowns. Pete Trammell caught two of the touchdown passes and Tony Clausen caught one. Tony also threw a 24 yard touchdown pass to Sean Rinard. Jeremy Zavitz added two touchdown runs of five yards each. It was an up and down season which was just as we expected, especially with the difficult schedule we had. We finished 5-4 and did qualify for the state playoffs, but unfortunately had to play Muskegon in the first round. They were undefeated and won the state title that year.

2004-2006

In our first four years at Jenison, we averaged 7.5 wins per season and over 30 points per game. We had success winning the conference championship, qualifying for the state playoffs four years in a row, making it to the state championship game and more. In the next four years we would have one winning record. The talent level was way down from previous years and one year we only had 27 players due to low numbers of players in the junior and senior classes. Both of those back to back classes had low numbers throughout high school, so we knew that lower numbers were coming. In 2004 we were 4-5. In our five losses, we averaged less than six points per game. In two of the games, we did not even score, and gave up an average of 37 points per game. As a coach, you are always seeking ways to improve yourself, your staff and your team. We were running the same system we'd been running in the past and coaching the same way we always had, but we were not having the same success. It was extremely frustrating for me, our staff and our team. In 2005 we were 5-4 and very inconsistent. In our five wins, we won three games by an average of only five points and the other two by an average of 39 points. Once again this year, we not only had trouble scoring, but just moving the ball effectively on offense. Even though we were not winning as much as previous years, I still loved going to practice and working with the young men we had on our team. They remained positive, always gave their best effort and never gave up and I was very proud of them for that. I know our team, parents and fans wished we would have won more games, but nobody wanted to win more than I did.

In 2006 we ended up 2-7, but our guys played their hearts out every game. Again, we were not as talented as the teams we were playing, which was not a good situation to be in when we play in one of the toughest football conferences in the state. I knew that we would be in for a tough few years based on the records that our freshman and junior varsity teams were having in previous seasons. There would be no easy wins this season. In our seven losses, we averaged only ten points per game, while giving up about thirty per game. As the head coach, I was always trying to keep our players and staff motivated in spite of losing records. It was awesome to see our players and staff show up for every meeting, practice and game with optimism and excitement. Although we had not won many games in recent years, I continued to visit college staffs in the off-season, attend several clinics, carefully analyze our game tapes and work with our players in the offseason to keep that competitive edge. As the losses piled up, the past few seasons were very tough to take and were very difficult on me personally. If we had losing records in most of my seasons as a head coach, I don't think I would have continued coaching. I am a competitor and I hate to lose. I am not a sore loser, but it tears me up inside to lose and I take it personally. I had to heed the advice that I had preached to all of my teams about winning not being the most important thing, but giving your best effort was. I had been giving my best effort and I felt that our coaches were also. After having great success at Jenison High School in years prior, as well as at Flint Carman-Ainsworth and Grayling, it was gut wrenching to not have that same success in these past few years.

2007

We were finally expecting improvement this year. Although we did not have great talent, our staff felt that we now had enough talent to be more competitive than the previous few years. There was an excitement within our program, looking forward to this season. I was always looking for an opportunity to improve our program so I had organized a team camp in beautiful Leelanau County about three hours away in Northwest

Michigan. We had always put on a team camp, many times the largest in the state, but never like this. We stayed in cabins, practiced, ate and took in the sights together as a team. We worked on team building and developing the unity it would take to have a great season. When we finished the camp, I felt is was all worthwhile. I loved coaching those guys, we were developing a great team unity and all of us coaches and players were optimistic for the upcoming season.

We started off the season with two wins, which added to our pre season optimism. The following week, we had seven starters suspended the night before our third game. While we were practicing on Thursday, our high school principal walked out and named the seven players he wanted to see immediately. He briefly explained that none of them would play in our game the next night and many of them would miss more games. The suspensions given by the administration were a result of the players drinking at a party weeks earlier. Due to the short notice, we had no time to prepare all of the back up players for our game the next night. With these suspensions along with some injuries, we played the rest of the season with players that were not nearly as good as the competition we faced and the unity of the team had been fractured with the suspensions. We never recovered and lost our last seven games. As a result, I was asked to resign or be fired after the season ended. The superintendent felt that a coaching change was the answer. Over the next seven seasons after I left, Jension had three different head coaches and averaged only one win per season. One of those coaches went on to win a couple of state championships at another school. We're all better coaches when we have better talent.

As I mentioned in an earlier chapter, this was a very difficult time for me and my family. One of the hardest things I have ever had to do was come home and sit down with my wife and two kids to explain that I was no longer wanted as the head football coach. I was embarrassed. With tears dripping down my cheeks, I explained why their father and husband was no longer wanted as the head coach. At the time, my oldest daughter, Laura had just gotten married the previous June. She had been out of the house for several years, so it would not affect her as much as it would Lyndsay and Luke. Fortunately, Lyndsay and Luke were not in high school yet. But, at ages 12 and 11, they had to deal with questions and taunts from some of their young classmates. I could handle people saying mean things to me, but I had a very difficult time with some of the teasing my kids had to deal with. It was only a few kids as their best friends would never say anything to hurt them. I was hurting not only because I got fired but was now hurting for what my kids had to endure. I was still in disbelief that I got fired. I felt like it was utterly unfair since I did not do anything wrong. Granted, we had not had the success in recent seasons as we did the first several years at Jenison, but I was not coaching in the NFL, it is high school football.

CHAPTER 14

WE'RE ALL BETTER COACHES WHEN WE HAVE BETTER TALENT

The bounce of a football is very unpredictable, just like coaching. Our coaching staff at Jenison High School did not go from being good coaches with previous successful seasons, to bad coaches that do not know what they are doing overnight. Whether we coached a team with a winning record, a losing record, a championship team, a playoff team or a team playing for the state championship, we coached every team the same. In fact, we thought that many times we did a better job of coaching when we had less talent and losing records than the years we had more success. When coaches have teams with less talent, you have to pay more attention to detail, fundamentals and many times simplify things, which forces you to be a better coach. It's easy to coach a talented team. Talented players make all of us look like better coaches. I've known several great coaches who had losing seasons and it certainly wasn't because of their lack of knowledge, commitment or enthusiasm. Too many times, we as coaches get too much credit when we win and many times too much criticism when we lose. Getting players to compete at their highest level is what's most important. If that's good enough to win games, great. If it's not, that's OK too. They can't give any more than their best effort. Our coaches were doing the best they could to get the most out of each player. When the season doesn't work out as well as you'd hoped, it's only natural for coaches to self evaluate and find ways to improve, especially when working with less talented players. Even though our system and coaching techniques had worked fine in the past with better talent, it was very frustrating now losing more games, scoring far fewer points and giving up far more points.

In the NFL or at major colleges, football is a big business. Firings are common and accepted as a part of the coaching profession if the coaches could not win enough games. In high school football, we do not have the ability to recruit players, we play with the young men that live in our school district and who choose to be on the team. If you coach long enough, it is understood that some years you simply have better talent than others. There are many great high school coaches in the country that did not win championships and had losing records. They molded young men, instilled discipline, taught them to have a great work ethic and how to overcome adversity. I do not think that any high school coach should be fired for not winning enough games. As long as the coaches are knowledgable, prepared, and sincerely care about their players, they should be viewed as great coaches. The coaches I think that deserve to be fired are coaches who not putting in necessary time and effort to prepare their teams, or coaches who do something illegal.

I have always said to our players over the years that winning is not the most important aspect of football, but giving your best effort is. Our guys always gave their best effort. Some of those years, we just were not very good and were playing in one of the toughest conferences in the state. We were the smallest school based on enrollment, in our conference. Three of the schools had twice the number of students we did. Our players were getting recognized in other ways. Opposing coaches and officials routinely complimented us on how hard our guys played, that they never gave up and always showed great sportsmanship. That made me very proud and I always shared the comments with our team. In the last three years at Jenison our teams were recognized with the Michigan High School Football Coaches Association's "Steve Spicer Leadership Award", Cornerstone University's "Champions of Character Award", OK Red Conference Sportsmanship Award and twice had Academic All State Teams. Like at most schools, the fellow coaches tend to be some of your best friends. At Jenison High School, three of my assistants were my best friends. We spent time away from football with our wives and families. Matt Schuiteman and Steve Uganski had played and graduated from Jenison and both taught at the high school. Ryan Nelson had played at rival Rockford High School and also taught at the high school. These three guys were great coaches and great friends.

A good friend of mine, Tony Annese, is the current head coach at Ferris State University and was the coach at Jenison prior to me. I remember he had told me before I accepted the Jenison job back in 2000. He said, "You'll never have the best talent in the conference. Most teams will have better talent, but the kids will work hard". They did. Another good friend, Jerry Kill, former head coach at Minnesota, had told me about how people put too much emphasis on the schemes coaches use, but it really boils down to who has the best players. He said, "It's not the X's and the O's, it's the Jimmies and the Joes".

CHAPTER 15

PROUD DAD

Out of all my successes, being a dad has been my greatest success. I am so proud of my three kids Laura, Lyndsay and Luke. Also, I am extremely thankful for all of their support throughout my coaching career. All three are married now, but as they were growing up, were very proud that their dad was a head football coach. They all remember me putting in long hours during the season with meetings, practices and games. They all have vivid memories of me spending countless hours watching video tape as I spent my weekends and many evenings preparing for our next opponent. Many times they'd sit and watch with me. They'd ask questions about what I was looking for, why did I watch so much video and why did I keep rewinding every play so many times. As they got older and learned more about football, the questions became more specific. They'd want to know how I planned on attacking their defense, what coverages do they like to run in the defensive secondary and what plays will work best against them. They knew how much time I had to invest to properly prepare for each game and they were fine with that. Especially when they'd meet me on the field after a win after witnessing first hand the excitement from the fans and our players. My kids knew all of the players and the players all knew the Larkin kids. My two daughters both told me that they thought it would be so great being the head coach's daughter when they were in high school, thinking they'd have their pick of who they'd like to date. Both girls told me that it was more of a curse than anything as none of the players would ask them out because they were too afraid of me. We still get a good laugh about that to this day. My son, Luke looked up to our players and loved being around them at practices and games. They always made Luke feel welcome and part of the team. I've talked about my background and my career in this book, but since I've dedicated this book to them and the support they've given me, I'd like you to know a little more about each of them.

Laura, my oldest, lives in Flint, Michigan with her husband Jason along with my three grandkids, Landon, Charlotte and Aiden. Laura is a fantastic mother, wife and daughter. She's an excellent cook and one of the most caring people I know. Her husband, Jason is pastor of a church they planted together called Union Flint. Laura was born one month premature with underdeveloped lungs. She was in the neonatal unit on a ventilator. Being only able to reach through the small holes in her incubator to touch her little arms and legs, was one of the hardest things I've ever had to deal with. I couldn't hold her for several weeks. I felt so helpless as I watched my tough little girl fight to stay alive. Laura's mother, Debbe and I were divorced when Laura was only five years old. The following year, I got my first head coaching job at Grayling High School, which was two and a half hours away from her. Laura stayed with me every other weekend during the school year and as often as I could see her during holiday and summer breaks. This was a difficult time for me both as a first year head coach and recently divorced with my daughter living so far away. I made the best of it by seeing Laura as much as I could, driving five hours round trip twice on the weekends that she stayed with me. Even at her young age, I wanted her to know how much I loved her and that I would always be there for her. Laura was nine when I got the head coaching job at Flint Carman-Ainsworth and soon after she came to live with me. She attending Carman-Ainsworth schools from third through ninth grade until I got the head coaching job at Jenison High School. Although Laura didn't particularly like Math, she loved her ninth grade Algebra teacher and her tenth grade Geometry teacher...ME. It was very difficult for Laura to leave her friends in Flint and move across the state prior to her sophomore year. She didn't want to go initially, but fortunately she agreed and fit in perfectly making many new friends in Jenison while still keeping in touch with her friends back in Flint. Laura graduated from Jenison, then attended

Hope College. She worked hard in school, got good grades and was well liked by everyone that knew her. I've always been proud of Laura for being such a loving daughter and a caring friend to so many that knew her. I was most proud of the strong faith she had, which started as a young girl and has only gotten stronger as she is now married and the mother of my three grandkids. While living in an apartment at Hope College with some other girls, I had offered to come over to make them a big pot of my famous Seafood Gumbo. I love to cook and Laura has eaten my gumbo several times. When I suggested making them dinner, the girls were very excited. They loved the meal and I loved making it for them. Laura went on three mission trips while attending Hope College, the last one in her senior year to South Africa. I remember before that trip talking to Laura about how most of her girlfriends from high school and college were either already married, engaged or had a steady boyfriend. Laura expressed concern about not having found Mr. Right yet. I told her not to be concerned and that it will happen when she least expects it. Sure enough, I get a call from her in South Africa telling me that she has met the most amazing guy while riding the bus from the airport to a village they would be doing mission work. Laura was as excited as ever. Although I was happy for her, my first thought was that she'd fallen in love with a guy from South Africa and I will hardly ever see her if she decides to live there. Fortunately, she calmed me down and told me that the guy she met, Jason, was from the Chicago area and part of the mission trip as well. Needless to say, I was very relieved. They have been happily married ever since. I am so proud of the woman that Laura has become.

Lyndsay, my middle child, was born during my second year as the head coach at Carman-Ainsworth in Flint. We moved to Jenison when she was five, where she attended school through tenth grade. After moving to Grand Haven, Lyndsay went to high school there for her junior and senior year. Lyndsay has experienced the championships at Carman-Ainsworth, Jenison, Grand Valley State University and Grand Haven High School. She has also been there for my Hall of Fame induction, coaching the East-West All Star football game and a few Notre Dame football games, which we both loved. Lyndsay liked football at an early age, probably because she saw how much time I put into coaching and how much I enjoyed it. Her and I always had a special bond when it came to football. She'd love going to my games and being the first one to give me a big hug on the field afterwards. Many times after the game, she'd be right next to me, with my arm around her, as a local TV sports reporters would be interviewing me. Lyndsay would watch video tape with me of our next opponent always asking questions and eager to learn. As a result, to this day, she can carry on an in depth conversation with any football enthusiast about play calling, strategy, motivation, fundamentals and recruiting. When Lyndsay was in fourth grade, she wanted to play youth football in Jenison, where I was the head coach. It was a fully padded, tackle football league. When she first approached me about playing, I said no right away. I didn't want my little girl playing tackle football with all the guys and being the only girl in the league, I was concerned for her safety. Also, as the head football coach, I thought people in the community might think I was forcing my daughter to play. It was just the opposite. I was hoping she'd just give up hope and stop asking, but Lyndsay was persistent about wanting to play. This trait of setting her mind on something and pursuing it, is still with Lyndsay today. When I realized she wasn't backing down and I really didn't have a good reason to say no, I agreed to talk about the possibility of her playing a little more. I sat her down and asked her to give me one good reason why I should let her play. Lyndsay responded by saying, "I just want to hit somebody". How could I say no. I agreed to let her play. She loved it and I loved watching her. She was a tough, hard working team player that never gave up. A coach's dream. Lyndsay played on the soccer team at Jenison, but after moving to Grand Haven, she started playing lacrosse. During her freshman year at Jenison, I was teaching Physical Education and Reproductive Health. The students referred to Reproductive Health as "Sex Ed" and all freshman were required to take it. There was no way Lyndsay wanted her dad teaching her sex ed, so she strongly requested and got a female teacher. She was a two year starter on the varsity girls lacrosse team and team captain her senior year. I loved watching Lyndsay play because she was so intense. She reminded me of myself at that age. She signed a National Letter of Intent and received a lacrosse scholarship. Lyndsay decided not to play in college, but did come back to Grand Haven High School as an assistant coach for the girls lacrosse team, which she thoroughly enjoyed. She was just as intense, if not more, as a coach instead of a player. Lyndsay said that anytime somebody yelled out, "Coach Larkin", she'd turn around to see if I was there. We have so many great memories together of Lyndsay growing up. Family trips, boating, the beach, shooting her first deer, Chrysler Lebaron convertible for her 16th birthday and numerous football games. Her and I loved watching the movie "Remember The Titans" together. Just another football bonding moment between the two of us. In the movie, a young girl named Sheryl Yoast and daughter of a successful coach, was just like Lyndsay. She loved football, very intense about the sport and proud of her father's accomplishments. In one of her lines in the movie, the coach's daughter said, "I ain't gonna lie, I wanted the Hall of Fame real bad". Lyndsay and I have laughed about that one line ever since because she wanted to see her dad get inducted into the Michigan High School Football Coach's Association's Hall of Fame. When Lyndsay was fourteen, we got word that I was getting inducted. I know that nobody in the room of 500 guests at the Hall of Fame induction ceremony was more proud of me than my daughter, Lyndsay. Lyndsay is married to James and they live on 11.5 acres with dogs, cats, goats, chickens and ducks. She still likes watching football with her dad. I'm very proud of the woman and wife that Lyndsay has become.

Luke is my youngest and only son. Luke was born in October, right in the middle of football season when I was the head coach at Carman-Ainsworth. He doesn't remember much about living in Flint as he was only three years old when I left to became the head coach at Jenison High School. Luke and I have played a lot of catch with the football over the years. He loved playing football and watching it whenever he could. Luke was a quarterback in high school and one of the smartest ones I've ever coached. Luke was very competitive and would always give his best effort. He spent quite a bit of time watching video tape with me as a young boy and then even more when he was playing in high school. Luke has always been well liked. Everyone from his teachers, friends and their parents would comment on Luke's outgoing, happy personality. You'd rarely see him down. He always had a very positive outlook on life and truly liked being around other people. Like Lyndsay, who was only a year and a half older, Luke has fond memories of family trips, boating, the beach, hunting, fishing and lots of football games. One year when he was about ten years old, I took him to see a University of Michigan football game at The Big

House, a Michigan State University football game at Spartan Stadium and a Detroit Lions football game at Ford Field. Luke loved wearing football replica jerseys as a kid. In fact, he had so many, he could go to school for two weeks and not wear the same one twice. Of course he had UM, MSU and Lions jerseys to wear to the games. He realizes now how fortunate he was to see those three teams play all in the same season. Luke used to enjoy going out on our boat, but as he got older, he wanted to be on the beach at the state park with all the other teenagers. Luke had some great friends growing up in Grand Haven, which is a resort town on Lake Michigan. They all had mopeds and would ride all over town and all day long like a motorcycle gang. His friends all had great parents and we'd all look after the boys the best we could when they decided to stop at our houses. Luke's first vehicle was a blue Ford pick up truck that I drove for several years. He loved driving that truck. Luke had nicknames for everything and everyone, so it was only normal that he called his truck "Mohamed". One day while he and his friends were playing catch with the football, they all thought it would be fun to see who could throw it through the sliding window on the back of the cab. After one perfect pass, the windshield shattered. It was a costly lesson for Luke. Luke was very popular and well liked with a zest for living. His friends loved having Luke around because he was always laughing and having a good time. In high school he played quarterback on the football team and scrum half on the rugby team. On our way back from practices or at the house, we rarely talked football. I was just his dad, not coach then. I would purposely talk about other things like school, friends and plans he had. His senior year, as team captain, the Grand Haven rugby team made it to the state semi-finals. Also, during his senior year, Luke would participate in the Down Under Bowl, which is a football tournament in Australia. The tournament was only for graduated seniors and was composed of teams throughout the United States and Australia. I had been asked to be the head coach in the Down Under Bowl for the team representing the Great Lakes area eight years earlier. I accepted and our team was undefeated and won the gold medal. After declining to go back every year after that, I decided to accept the honor again and bring Luke with me to experience the football tournament and the cultural experience of Australia and Hawaii. With Luke as our quarterback and one of his best friends from Grand Haven, Jacob Kostner, as a wide receiver, we once again went undefeated and won the gold medal. Luke and Jacob both played exceptionally well and connected on several touchdown passes. Luke played so well that he was voted Most Valuable Offense Player for the Down Under Bowl by their committee and received a trophy for it, along with his gold medal. It was another great bonding time for Luke and I. Being his dad and his coach, I was extremely proud of Luke. One of my best friends,

Dave Stull, was my assistant coach for the Down Under Bowl. We both had a great time coaching our team and getting to know our players from all over the Great Lakes area. After graduating from high school, Luke went to Albion College to work on his business degree and play football. He enjoyed his experience there playing football and making new friends. After spring football practice, where they predicted him competing for a starting position, Luke called me to ask if I'd mind if he transferred to Davenport University to continue his business degree and play rugby. Davenport had offered Luke a rugby scholarship his senior year but he declined it to attend Albion College. He really missed playing rugby and Davenport had a very good team. Luke explained that he would still work on his business degree and be closer to home all while playing a sport he truly loved. He was worried that with me being a football coach my whole life, that I would rather him stay at Albion College. I told Luke that it's completely his decision. I just want him to be happy and that I would support any decision he made. It turned out to be a great decision. Luke graduated with honors and a business degree. He was a three year starter and major contributor to the rugby team. Most importantly spent those three years with his future wife, Terin, who was also getting a business degree and was on a tennis scholarship. I always tell Luke that he definitely "married up". I couldn't ask for a greater daughter-in-law than Terin. They too are happily married and they both continue with that zest for living. I'm very proud of what Luke has accomplished, but more importantly the kind of man he has become.

Like most coaches, I felt that my parenting style was much different than my coaching style. As the head football coach on Friday nights, I was very emotional, outgoing, animated and usually quite loud. As a father, I was much more calm, quiet and loving. With both my players and my kids, I expected their best, encouraged them, gave them a hug when they needed it and disciplined them when they deserved it. Laura and Lyndsay would ask me not to use my "coaching voice" at home, which I rarely did. I love my kids more than anything in the world. I've always tried to be there for them and always will. I would always encourage them to be kind and respectful to everyone they meet. All three of them are. I'm so proud of the way they turned out. If you asked any of my kids today what my favorite saying was, they would say, "Be nice to everyone. You can never have too many friends".

CHAPTER 16

TAKE A KNEE

At the end of every practice and every game, I wanted to give my players immediate feedback and summarize how I felt we did. I would always say, "take a knee". The players knew that meant to kneel on one knee together as a team and give me their complete attention. I would be standing in front of them as they were packed tightly together, so I could make eye contact with each player. I would quickly review the good and the bad, talk about improvements we must make and most importantly, tell the team how proud I was of them and their effort whether we won or lost.

So as I end this book, I'd like you to "take a knee" as I summarize what you read and emphasize the positives that I hope you take from it. Like every football clinic that I ever attended, I felt if I learned one thing, it was worth it. My hope is that you learned at least one thing from my experiences.

The purpose of this book is to share my experiences, philosophy, advice, inspiration and encouragement. Just like a football playbook is a step by step guide to keep you organized and on task, this "Coach's Playbook" is designed to do the same. I talked specifically about the importance of teamwork, unity and positive attitude. I've had my share of success and am very grateful for it. I'm not the most successful coach out there. This isn't about the perfect plan. This is about God's plan for my life. It was full of ups and downs. From championship seasons to losing seasons. From receiving numerous awards to being fired. Mine was a career that started coaching my younger brother and 35 years later, ended with coaching my only son. It was a career that I thank God for everyday. I can't imagine being anything other than a high school teacher and varsity football coach.

The many championships and awards were great, but the awesome experiences I was fortunate enough to have with the thousands of players I've had the pleasure to coach, is what made it all worthwhile. One message that was consistent to all of the teams I coached was that winning isn't the most important thing. Giving your best effort is. I want to again thank all the players that I've ever coached for sacrificing their time and effort. Also, a big thanks to all of the parents of players that I've coached for allowing me the opportunity to spend so much quality time with their sons. I treated them like they were my own. I especially want to thank my three kids, Laura, Lyndsay and Luke for their loving support for me to pursue the coaching career I loved.

Finally, of all the topics I addressed in this book, I feel the most important one for all of us whether it's in the game of football or the game of life, is overcoming adversity. Life isn't easy. In fact, life can be very hard. We all face adversity. It's not a matter of IF we're going to face problems, it's WHEN. Everyone experiences issues dealing with marriages, relationships, financial, children and jobs. What is most important is how we deal with those adversities. As you've read, I've told you about many that I had to overcome. Like you, I will have many more down the road. Have hope. Be positive. Life's too short. Enjoy every day. Tell those closest to you how much you love them. If you're reading this, you are alive. Smile. Be thankful for what you have, not what you don't have.

DAVE LARKIN BIO

Playing Experience

1972-1975	Mt. Morris High School	QB
1976-1979	Saginaw Valley State	QB

Varsity Assistant Experience

1980, 1983	Mt. Morris HS, Mt. Morris, MI
1981-1982	Taravella HS, Coral Springs, Fla
1985-1988	Carman-Ainsworth HS, Flint, MI
1989-1990	Powers Catholic HS, Flint, MI
2010-2013	Grand Haven HS, Grand Haven, MI

Head Varsity Coaching Experience

1991-1993   Grayling HS, Grayling, MI

- Great Northern Conference Champions
- MHSAA State Playoffs
- MHSFCA Regional Coach of the Year

1994-1999   Carman-Ainsworth HS, Flint, MI

- Big 9 Conference Champions
- MHSAA State Playoffs
- Flint Journal All Area Coach of the Year

- Big 9 Conference Coach of the Year
- Carman-Ainsworth Athletic Hall of Fame

2000-2007   Jenison HS, Jenison, MI

- OK Red Conference Champions
- MHSAA State Playoffs
- Grand Rapids Press All Area Coach of the Year
- Detroit Lions Coach of the Week
- Division 2 State Runner-Up
- Michigan High School Football Coaches Association Hall of Fame
- Michigan High School Coaches Association Hall of Fame
- Head Coach, West All Stars, East-West All Star Football Game
- Head Coach, "Down Under Bowl", Australia
- National High School Athletic Coaches Association, National HS Football Chairman
- Michigan High School Football Coaches Association, "Steve Spicer Leadership Award"
- OK Red Conference Team Sportsmanship Award
- Cornerstone University "Champions of Character Award"
- Academic All State Football Team
- Past President, Michigan High School Football Coaches Association
- Past President, Michigan High School Coaches Association

College Coaching Experience

2008-2009, 2014   Grand Valley State University

- 2008,2014 Tight Ends
- 2009 Running Backs
- GLIAC Conference Champions
- NCAA Division II National Playoffs

Printed in the United States
by Baker & Taylor Publisher Services